EASY
Guitar Chords

by Jay Friedman

E - LOW
A
D
G
B
E - HIGH

©Copyright MCMLXXXIV by Lucky One Music Publications, Inc.
©Copyright assigned MCMLXXXVI Alfred Publishing Co., Inc.
All rights reserved. Printed in USA.

INTRODUCTION

In order to have a complete understanding of guitar chords, it is important to start with a solid knowledge of **all** the basic "open chords" (chords with at least one open string). ***Easy Guitar Chords*** gives you that chord foundation to build on.

All of the chords in this book are related to each other in such a way as to make them easy to remember. After each section, the chords are shown in a progression (order of chords) as they would be in a song. ***Easy Guitar Chords*** has all the chord knowledge you need to start playing the guitar.

So let's get started.

TABLE OF CONTENTS

MAJOR OPEN CHORDS
- E, A, D 4
- Testing the Chord 5
- Chord Changing 5
- G, C 6
- Major Chord Progressions 7

MINOR OPEN CHORDS
- Em, Am, Dm 9
- Relating the Major and Minor Chords 10
- Major and Minor Chord Progressions 11

DOMINANT SEVENTH OPEN CHORDS
- E7, A7, D7 13
- Chord Families (Relating Major, Minor and Seventh) 14
- G7, C7, B7 15
- Dominant Seventh Chord Progressions 16

MAJOR SEVENTH OPEN CHORDS
- Emaj7, Amaj7, Dmaj7, Gmaj7, Cmaj7 18
- Chord Review 19
- Fmaj7 20
- Major Seventh Chord Progressions 20

MINOR SEVENTH OPEN CHORDS
- Em7, Am7, Dm7 21
- Minor Seventh Chord Progressions 22

MAJOR SIXTH OPEN CHORDS
- E6, A6, D6, G6, C6 23
- Major Sixth Chord Progressions 24

MINOR SIXTH OPEN CHORDS
- Em6, Am6, Dm6 25
- Chord Review 26
- Minor Sixth Chord Progressions 27

NINTH OPEN CHORDS
- Add9 Chords 28
- Add9 Chord Progressions 29
- Dominant Ninth Chords 30
- Dominant Ninth Chord Progressions 32

SUSPENDED OPEN CHORDS
- Esus, Asus, Dsus, Gsus 33
- Relating Major and Suspended Chords 34
- Dominant Seventh Suspended Chords 35
- Suspended Chord Progressions 37

DIMINISHED OPEN CHORDS 38

AUGMENTED OPEN CHORDS 39

MASTER CHORD REVIEW (Chord Families) 41

RIGHT-HAND RHYTHM STRUMS 42

"OPEN CHORD" PROGRESSIONS 45

BASIC CHORD THEORY (What the Numbers Mean) 46

MAJOR OPEN CHORDS

E, A, and **D** are the three most basic chords played on the guitar.
Let's play them.

The "**O**" means to play the string open.
(No left-hand finger)

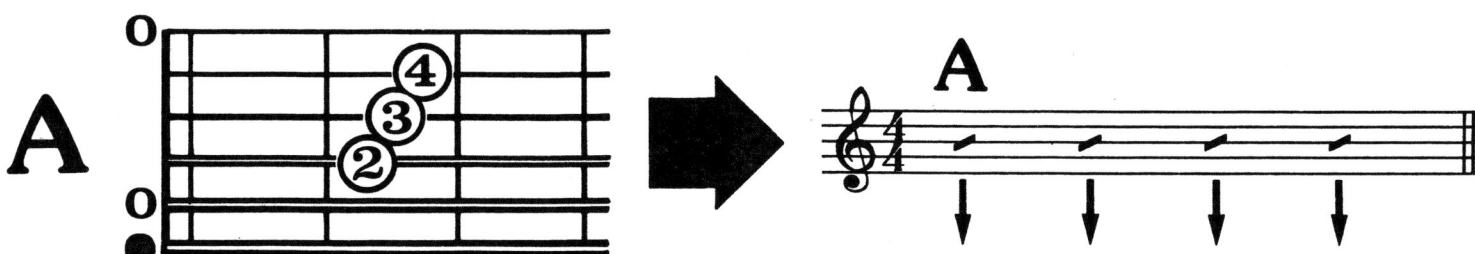

STRUM DOWN
(4 times)

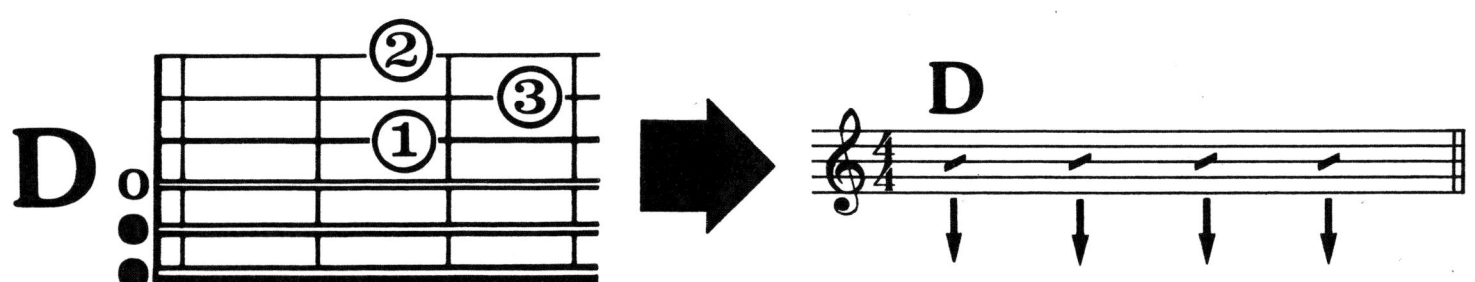

The "●" means **don't** play that string.
For the **A** chord-
Start each strum on the 5th string.

For the **D** chord-
Start each strum on the 4th string.

TESTING THE CHORD

How do these chords sound? As you strum across the strings, does each note of the chord sound clean and clear?

Test the chord by playing each note of the chord, one at a time. Make sure that-

-you are arching your left-hand fingers.
-you are using your **fingertips.**
-you are applying enough pressure to make the string sound.
-there are no fingers overlapping, touching the wrong string.
-your fingertips are between the metal frets, not on them.
-your thumb is in position behind the neck.

CHORD CHANGING

Once you can play the chords clearly, the next step is to change from one chord to another, as smoothly as possible.

To make chord changing easier, picture the next chord **before** you play it. Then move each finger the shortest distance needed to make the chord change. Now play through the following **chord changes.**

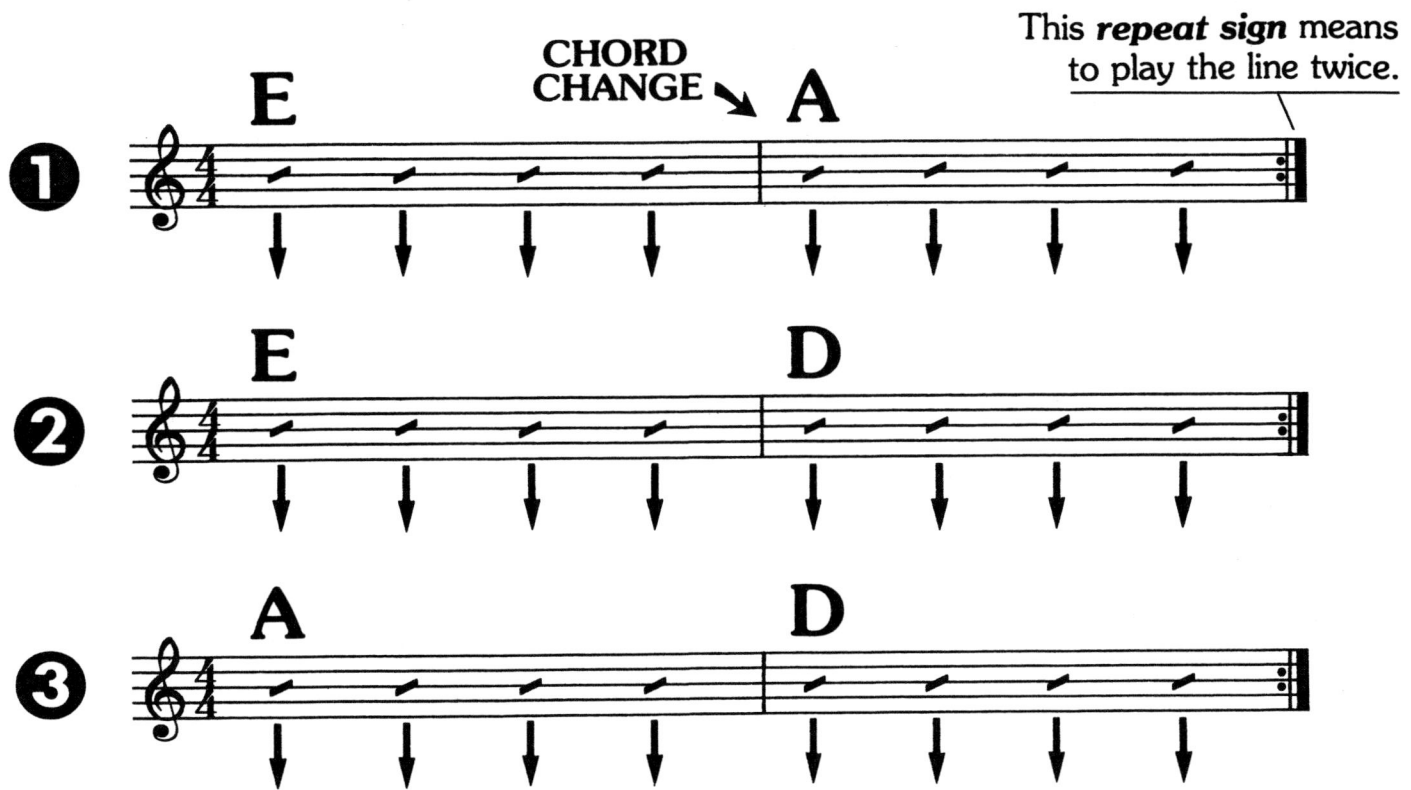

MORE MAJOR CHORDS
(G and C)

There are two more Major open chords: *G* and *C*.

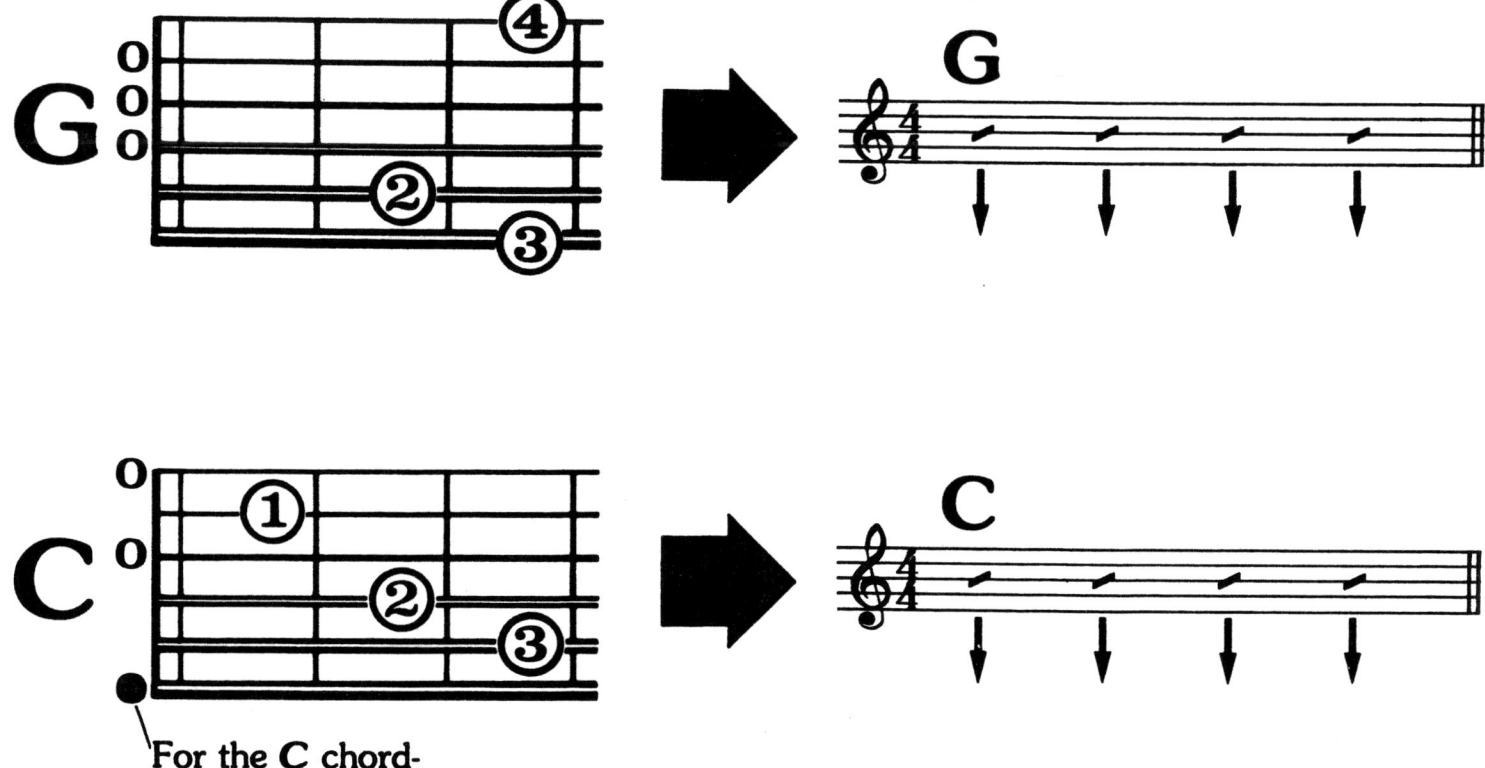

For the C chord-
Don't play the 6th string.
Start each strum on the 5th string.

The G and C chords are usually played together like this-

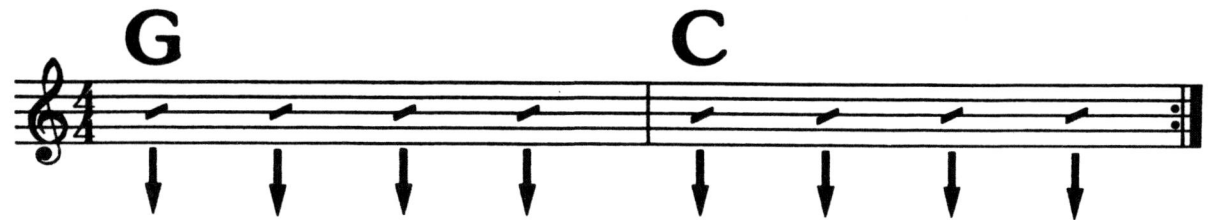

MAJOR CHORD PROGRESSIONS

E, A, D, G, and C are the five Major open
chords which all other chords will be related to.

Play these chord progressions slowly and evenly, using all of the five Major chords.
Be sure that you are playing the proper strings for each chord.

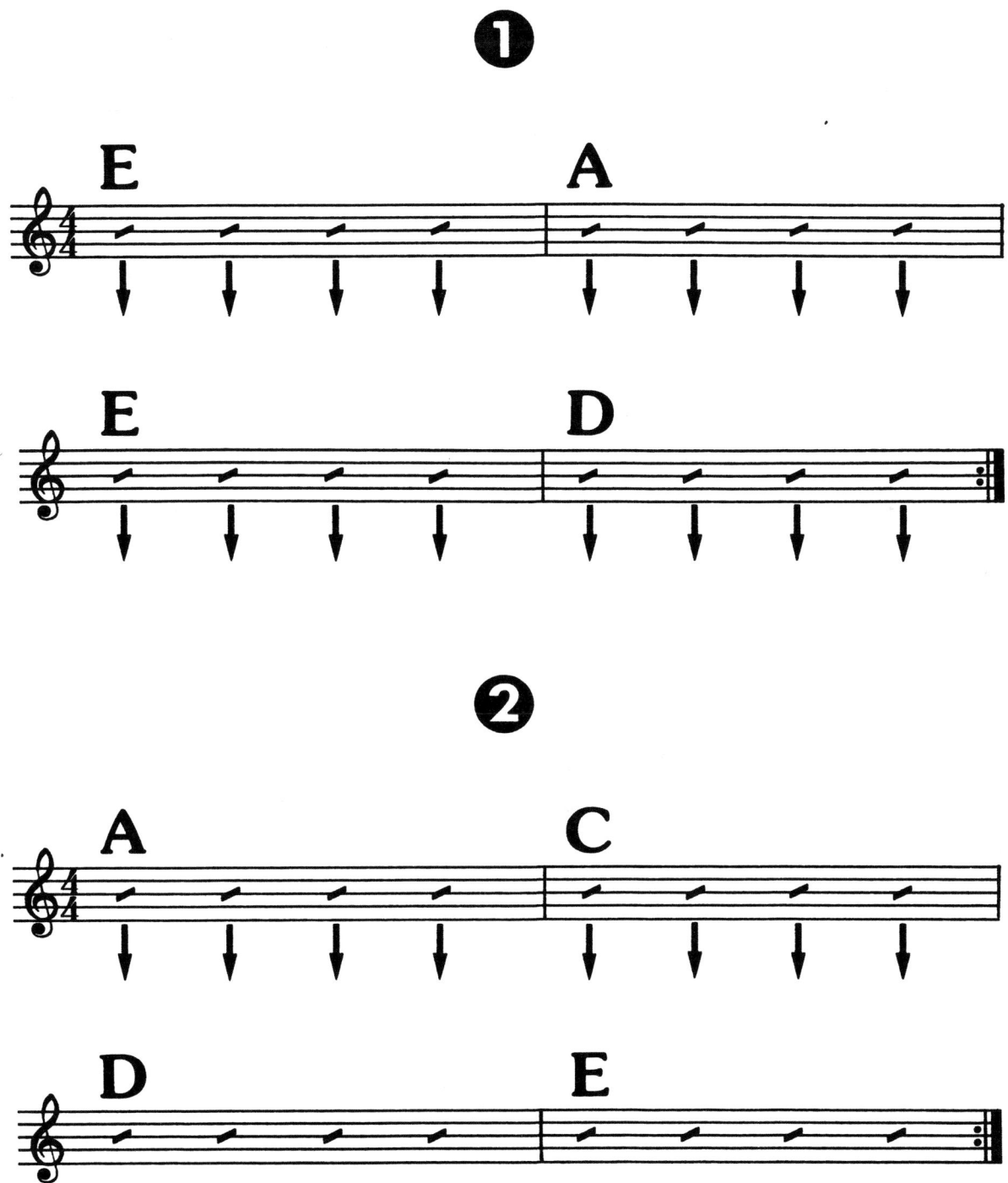

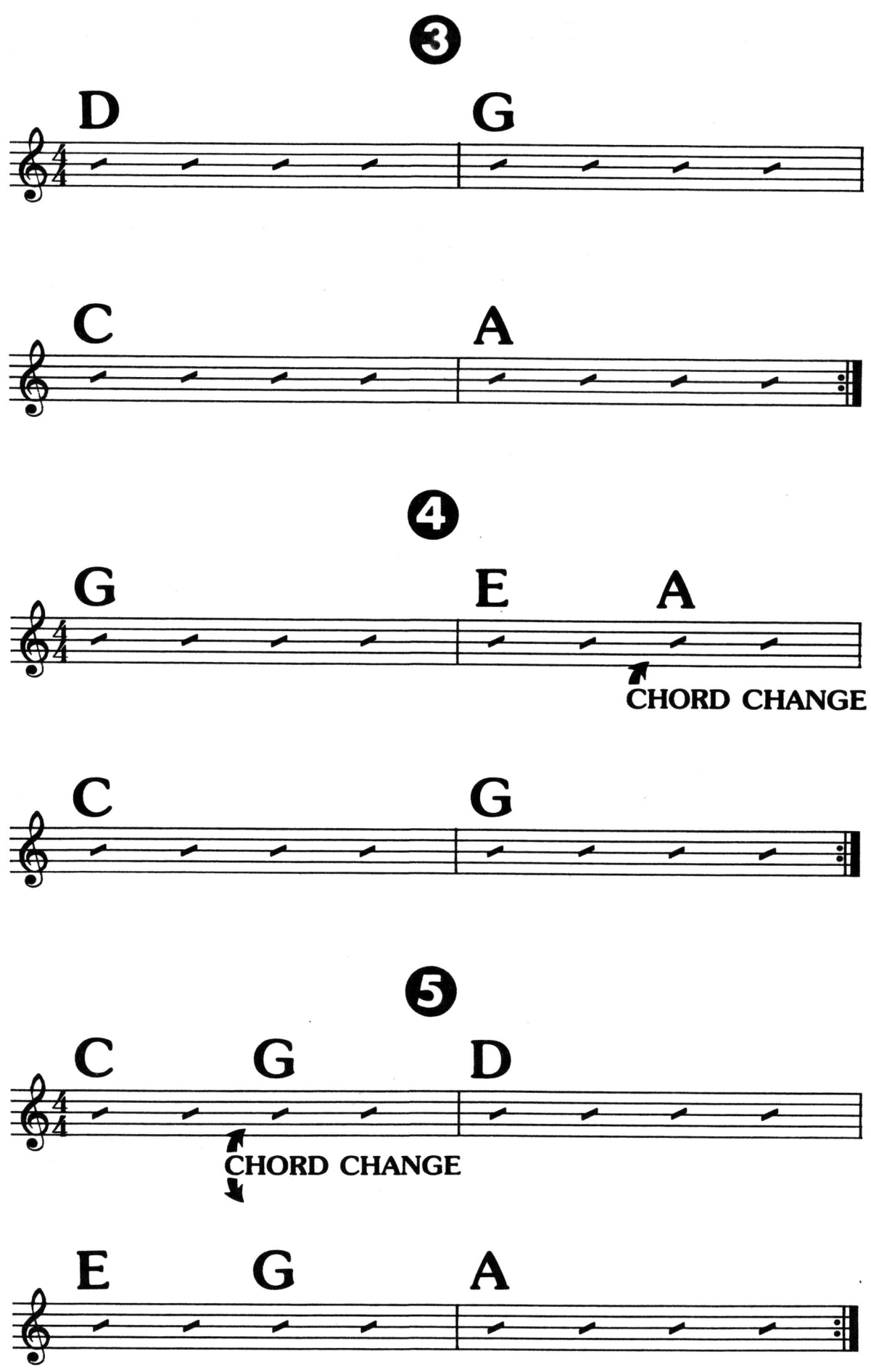

(For possible strums, turn to page 42.)

MINOR OPEN CHORDS

An "m" is the symbol for Minor.

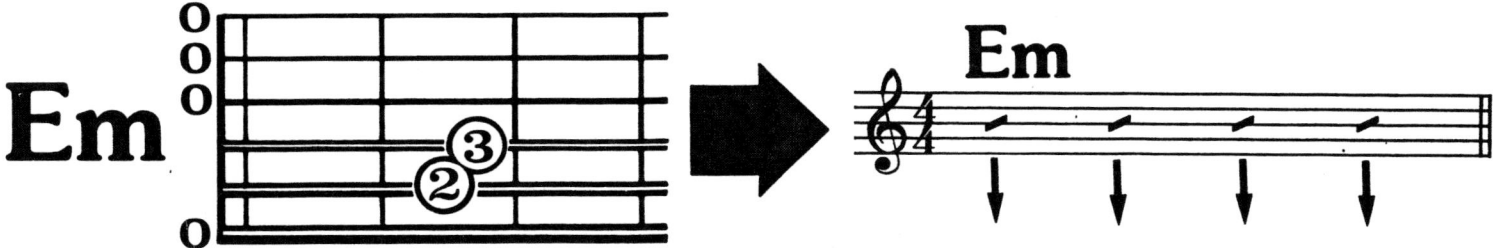

For the **Am** chord-
Don't play the 6th string.
Start each strum on the 5th string.

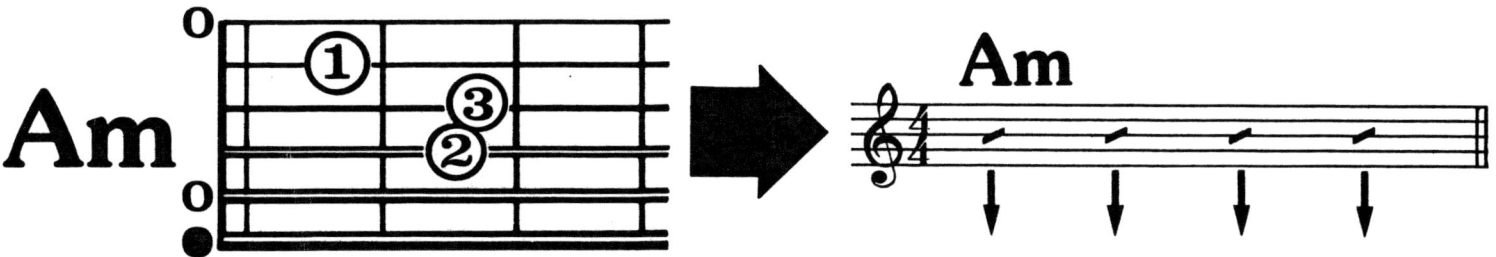

For the **Dm** chord-
Don't play the 5th and 6th string.
Start each strum on the 4th string.

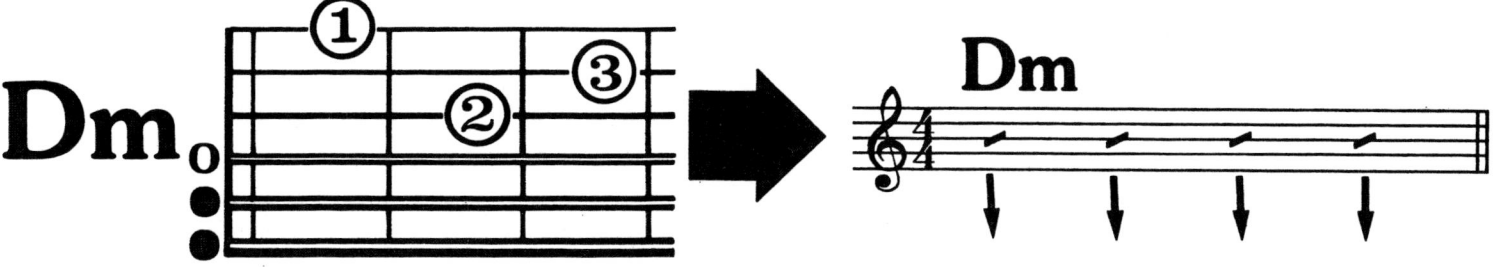

Repeat this Minor chord progression until you know the chords.

RELATING THE MAJOR AND MINOR CHORDS

Notice that only one note has changed to form each related Minor chord.

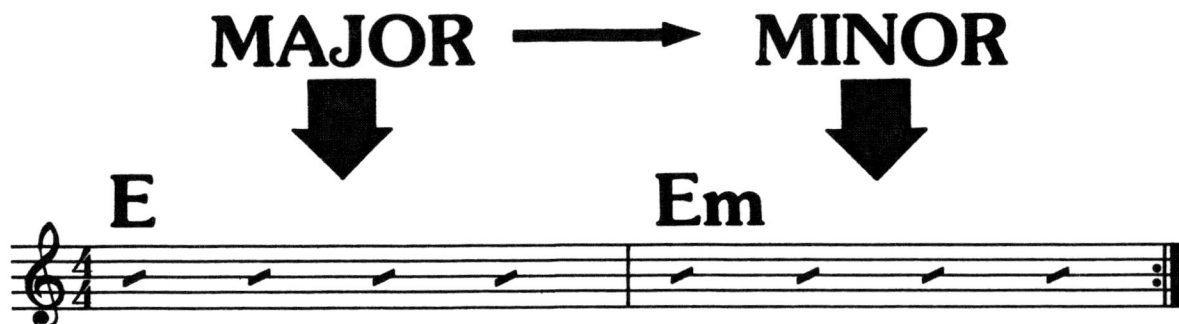

MAJOR AND MINOR CHORD PROGRESSIONS

Now let's put all of the Major and Minor chords together in a common chord progression.

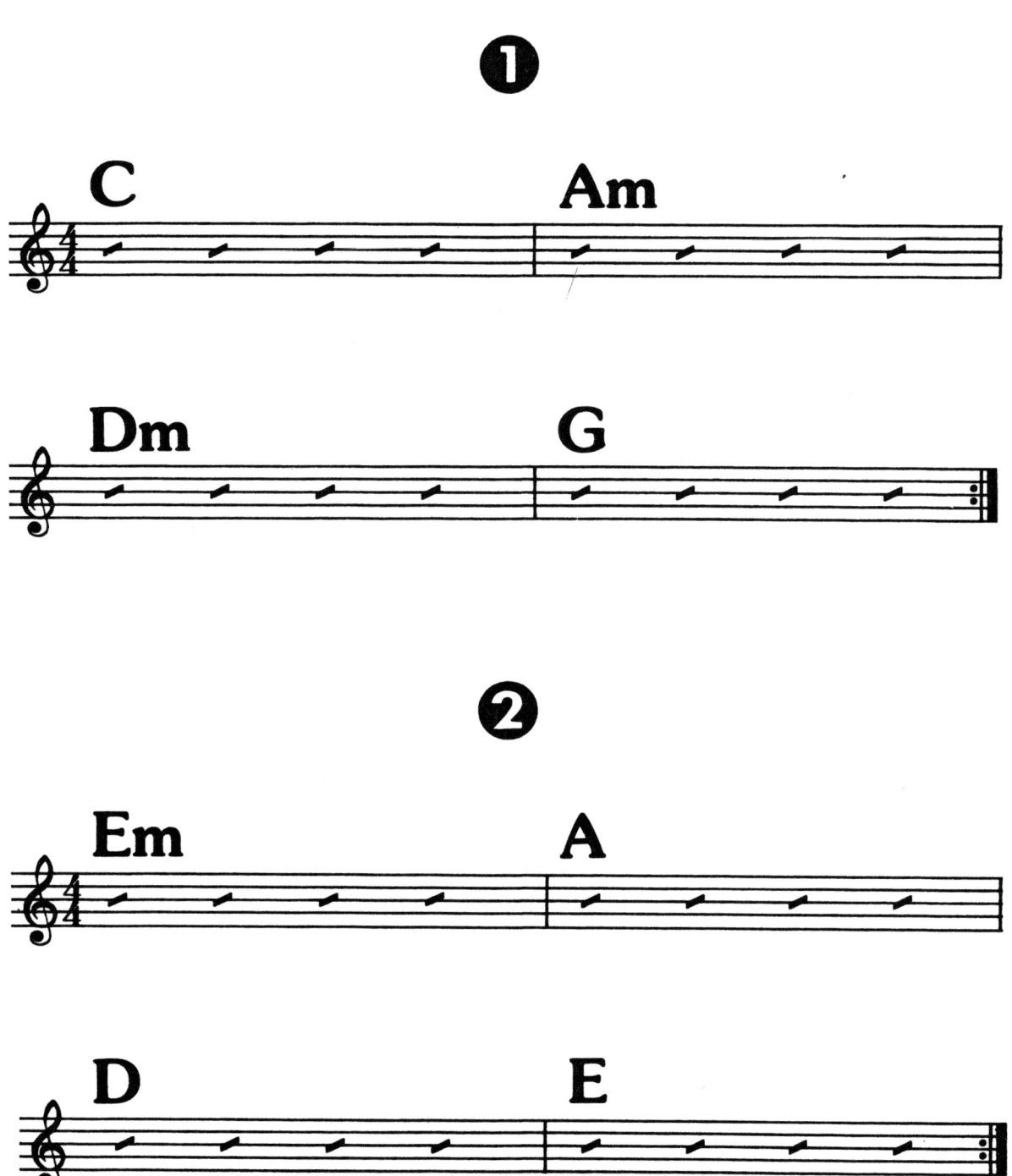

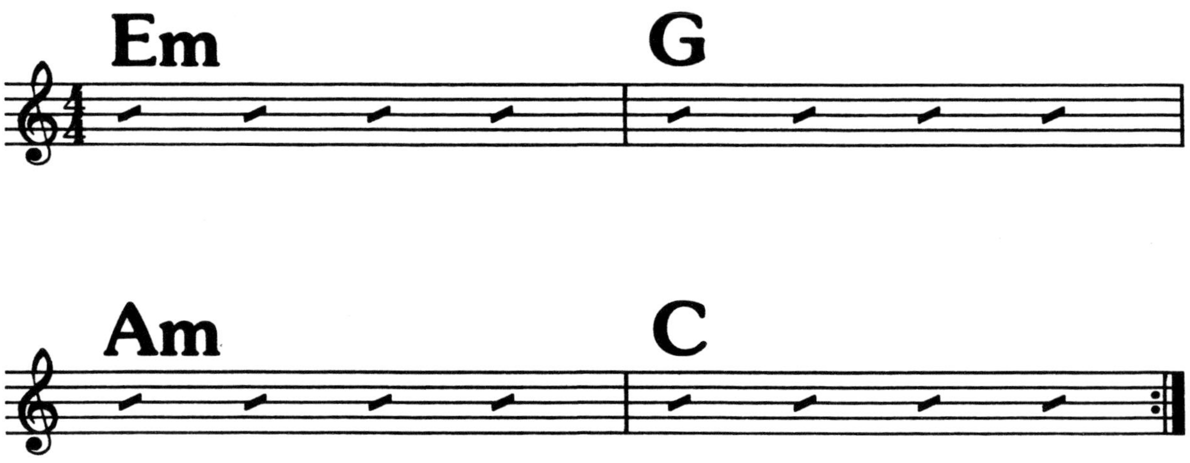

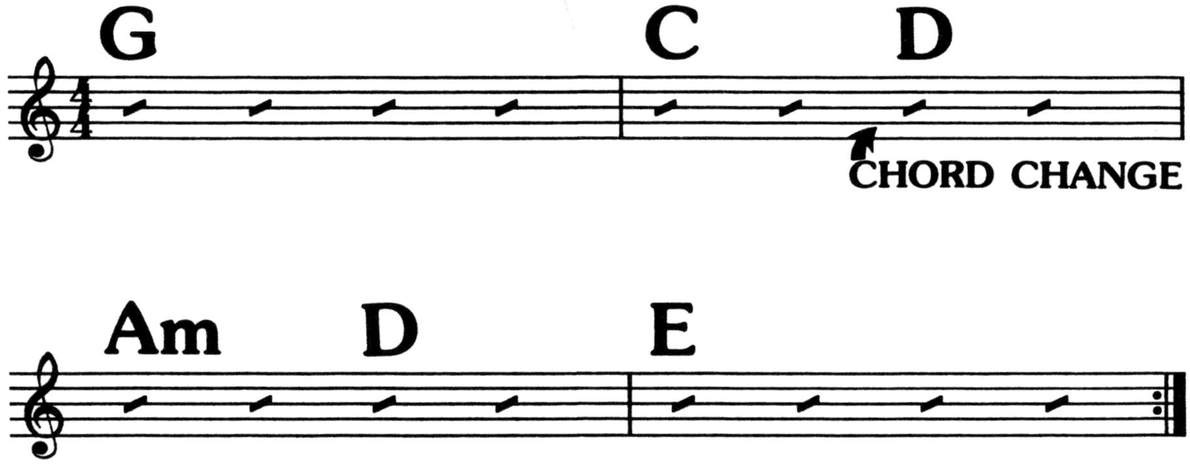

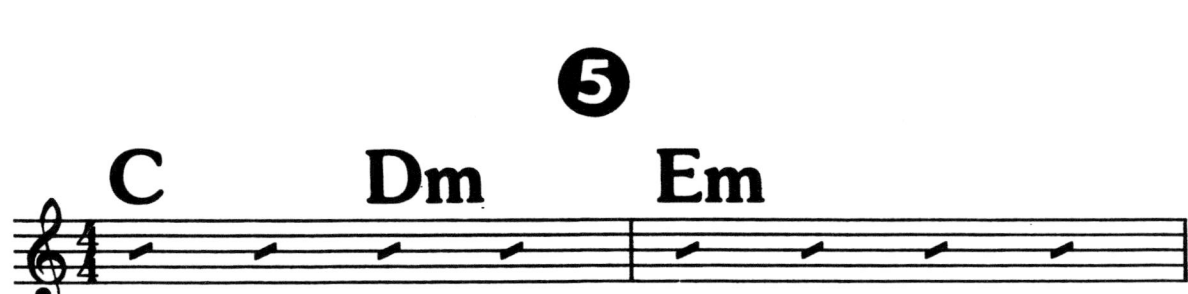

DOMINANT SEVENTH OPEN CHORDS

The number "7" is the symbol for the Dominant Seventh chord.

Start each **A7** strum on the 5th string.

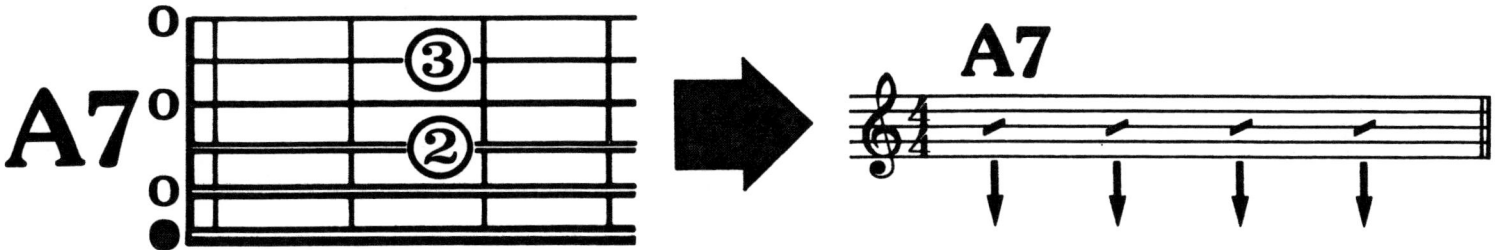

Start each **D7** strum on the 4th string.

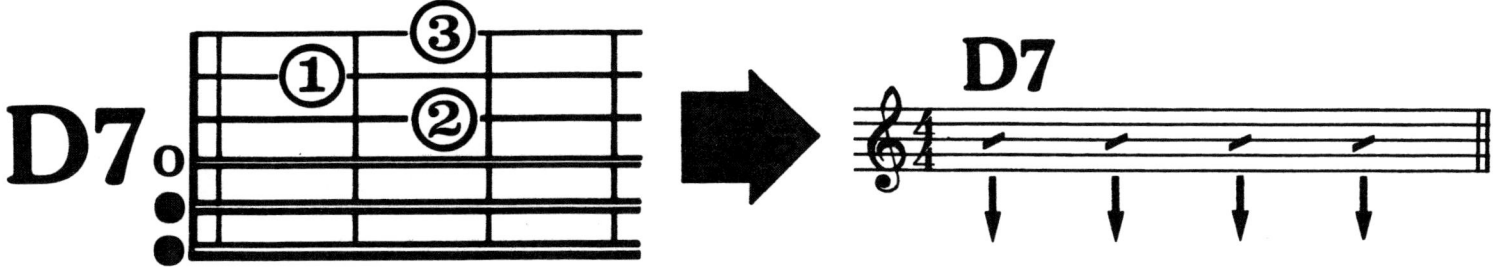

13

CHORD FAMILIES
RELATING THE MAJOR, MINOR, AND DOMINANT SEVENTH CHORDS

As we learn each new type of chord (Major, Minor, Dominant Seventh), we are building a bigger family in each key (E, A, D, etc.). Play through these progressions and you will see how similar the chords are in each chord family.

THE "E" CHORD FAMILY

THE "A" CHORD FAMILY

THE "D" CHORD FAMILY

MORE DOMINANT SEVENTH CHORDS
(G7, C7, and B7)

Here are **G7** and **C7**. They did not have Minor open chord positions.

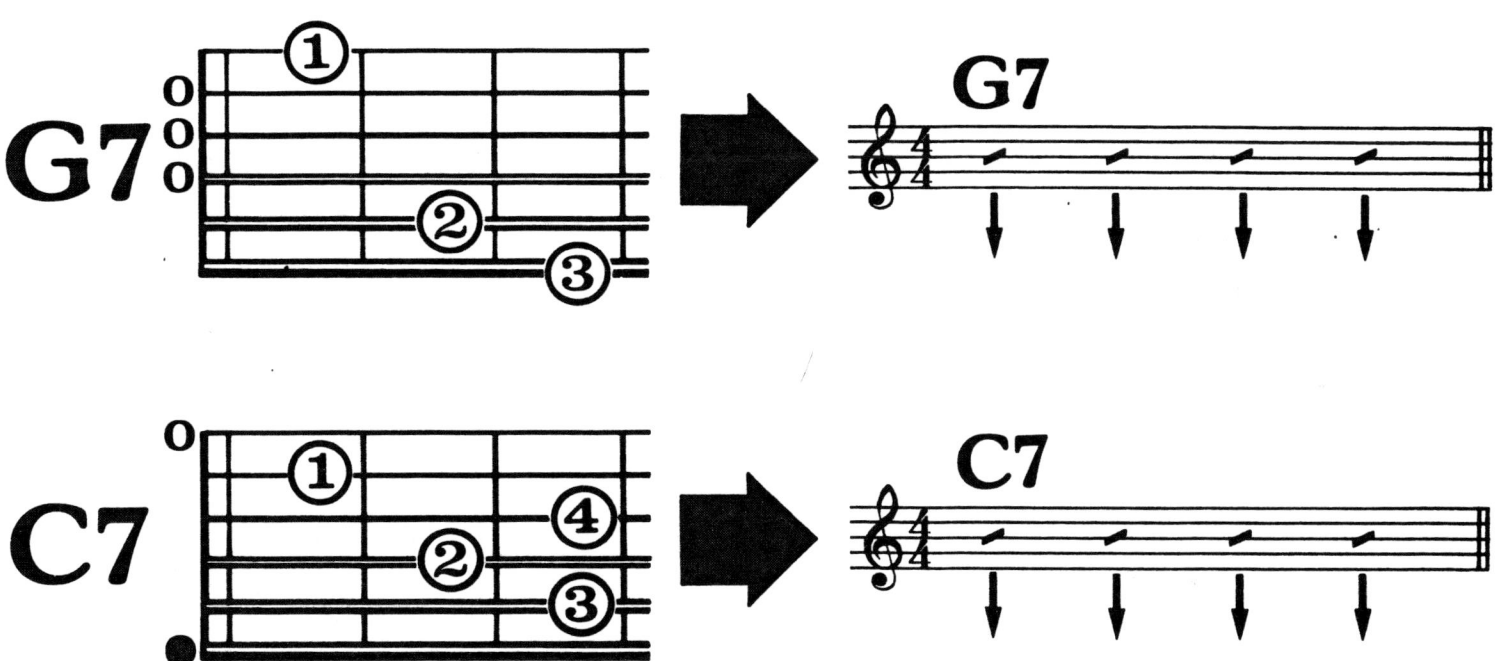

Notice how these chords relate to their Major counterpart-

Keep the 2nd and 3rd fingers in place through both chords.

Keep the C chord fingers down and add the 4th finger to get C7.

B7 is a one-of-a-kind chord. It is an important chord to know, even though it doesn't relate directly to one of the chord families we've discussed.

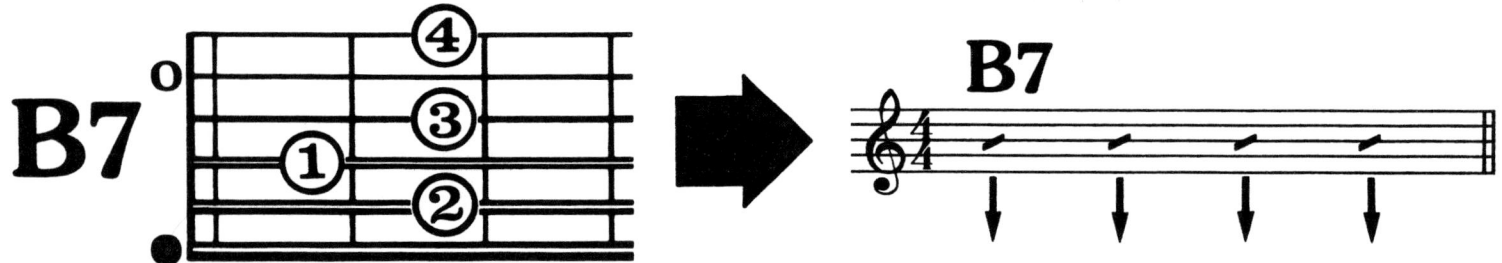

CHORD REVIEW

Play through this list of chords before you play the progressions to be sure that you know all of the chords so far.

E	A	D	G	C	
Em	Am	Dm			
E7	A7	D7	G7	C7	B7

DOMINANT SEVENTH CHORD PROGRESSIONS

Here are a few common chord progressions using the Dominant Seventh chords.

MAJOR SEVENTH OPEN CHORDS

"maj7" is the symbol for Major Seventh chords.

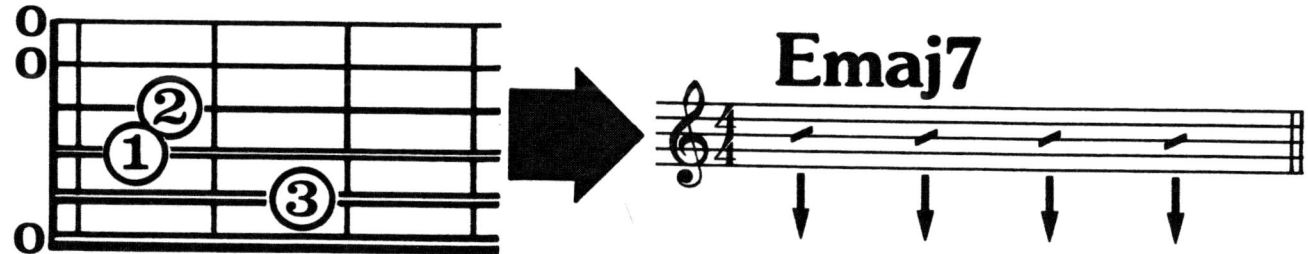

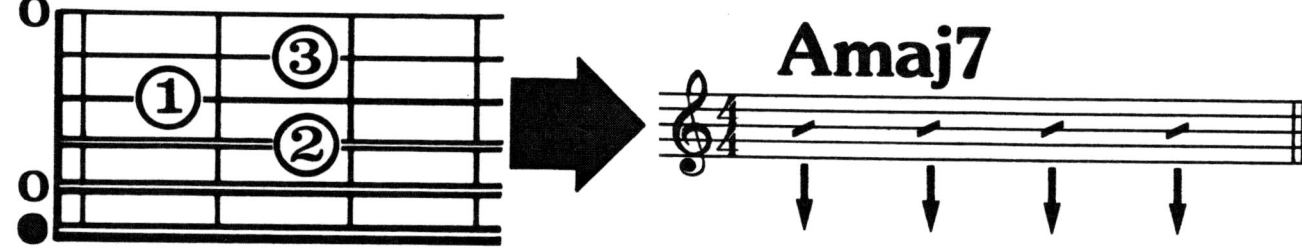

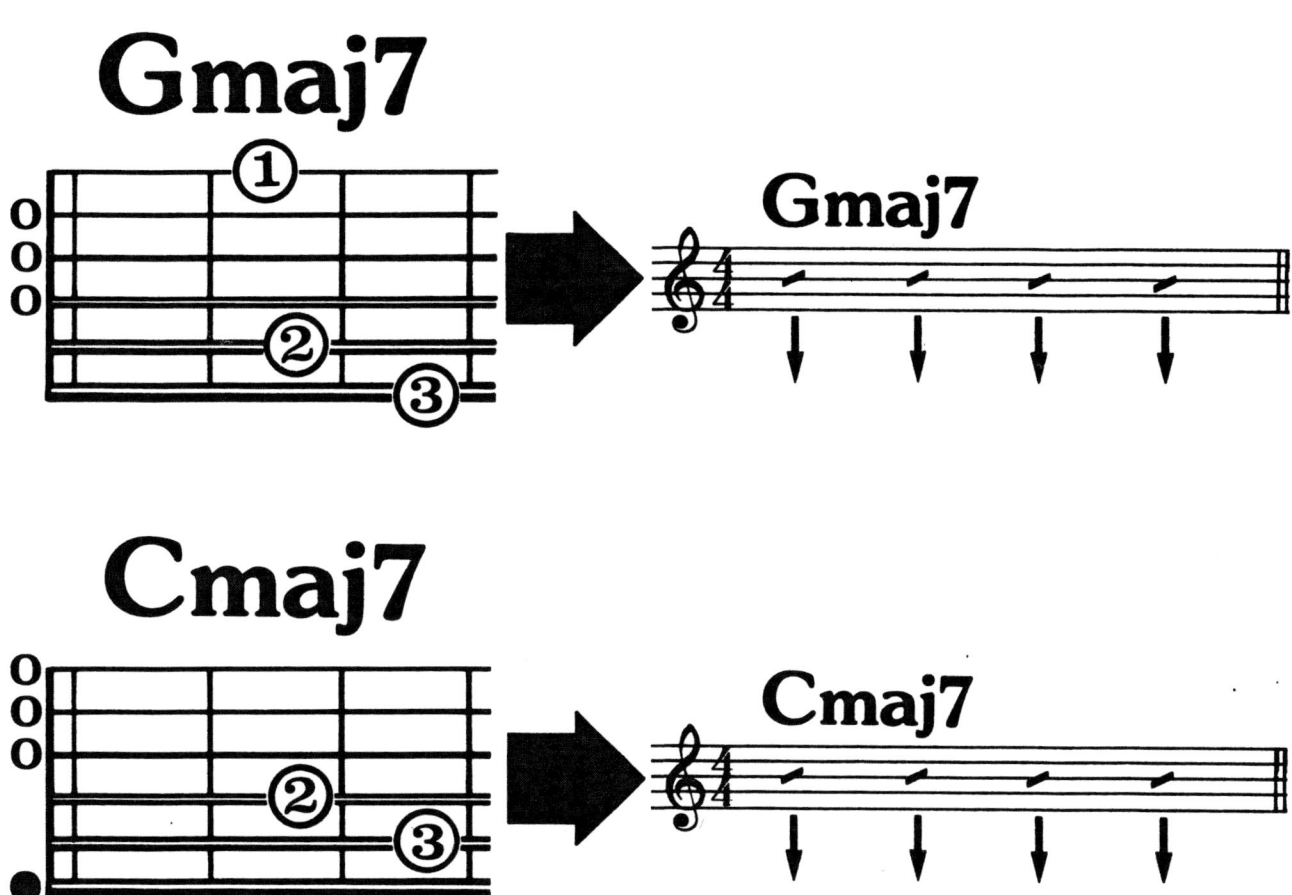

CHORD REVIEW

Once you've gone through the Major Seventh chords, add them to their related chord families. This will help you remember them.

E➡	E	Em	E7	Emaj7
A➡	A	Am	A7	Amaj7
D➡	D	Dm	D7	Dmaj7
G➡	G	-	G7	Gmaj7
C➡	C	-	C7	Cmaj7
(B)➡			B7	

As you are playing across each line, notice the similarity between each chord family member.

Fmaj7 is another one-of-a-kind chord (like B7 was).

MAJOR SEVENTH CHORD PROGRESSIONS

Notice that the chord changes are not only one each measure. Sometimes there are two chords in a measure.

MINOR SEVENTH OPEN CHORDS

The Minor Seventh chord is made by combining the Minor and the Dominant Seventh chords.

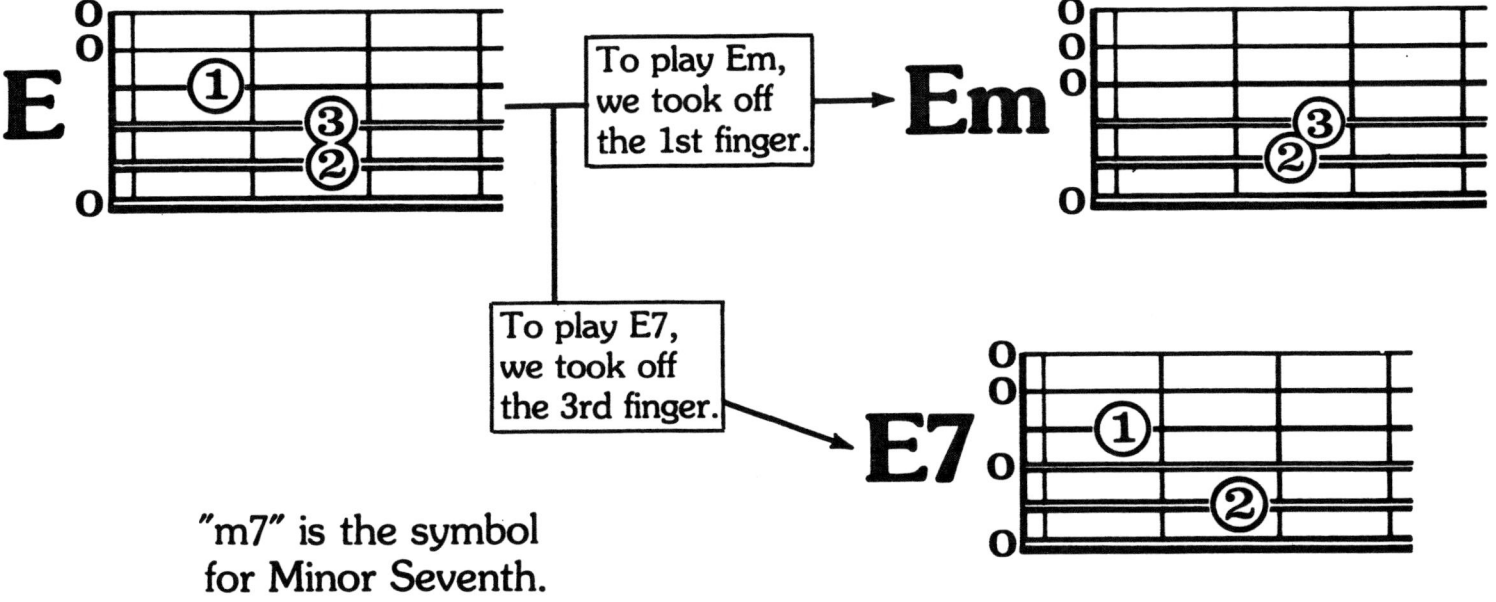

"m7" is the symbol for Minor Seventh.

To play **Em7**, take off the 1st finger (making it Minor) and take off the 3rd finger (making it a Dominant Seventh).

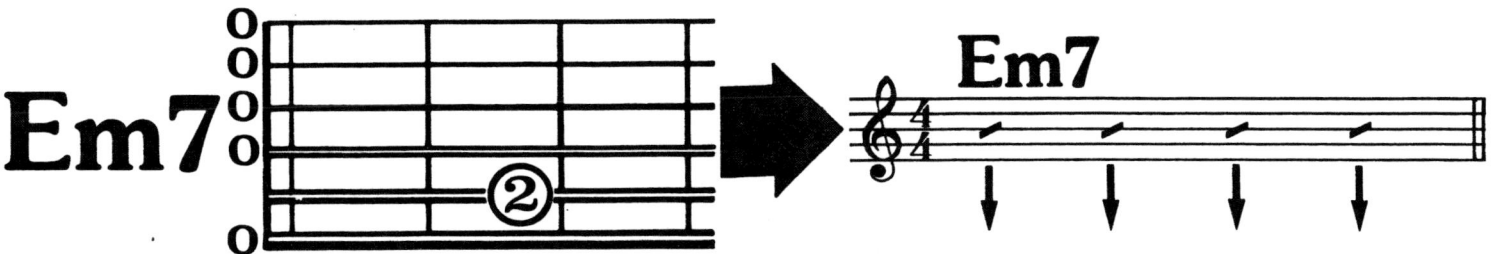

Using this same logic, try to figure out **Am7** and **Dm7** before looking at the chord diagrams. If you can, they will be easier to remember.

After you've tried, check your answers. ⇨

21

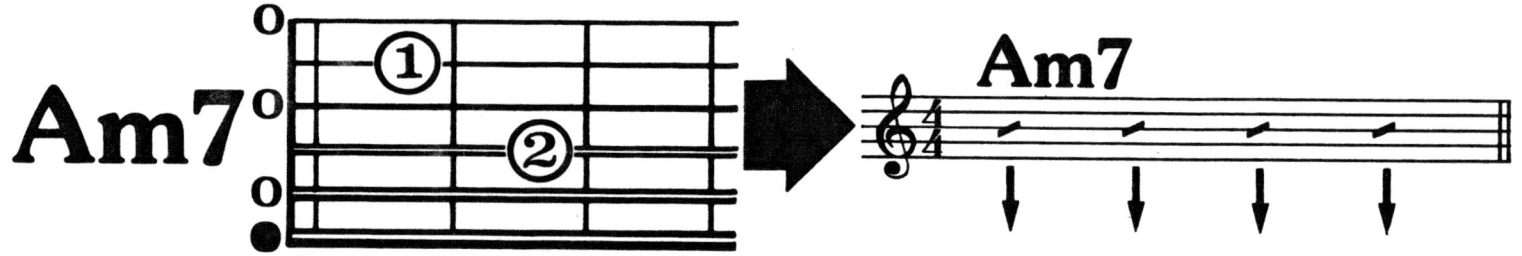

Lay the first finger across both strings.

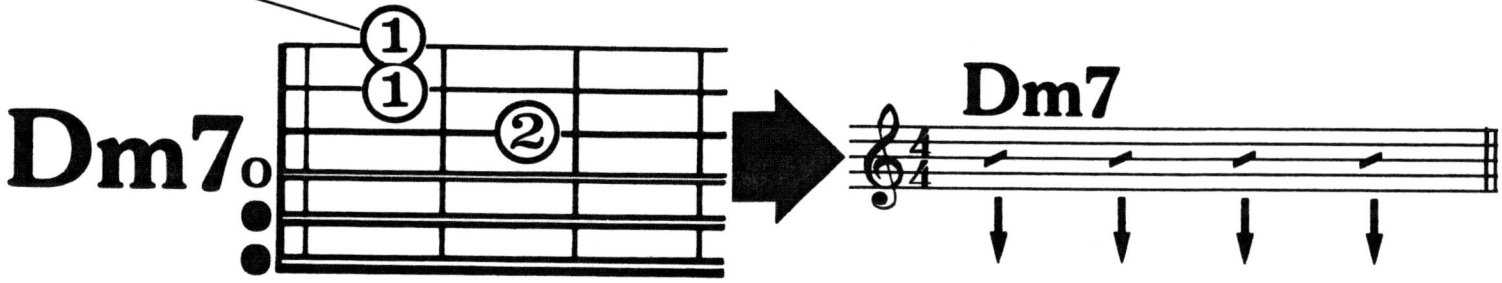

Are you *testing* each new chord? You should be.

MINOR SEVENTH CHORD PROGRESSIONS

MAJOR SIXTH OPEN CHORDS

The number "6" is the symbol for a Sixth chord.

Here are the Major Sixth chords which relate to the five Major chord families.

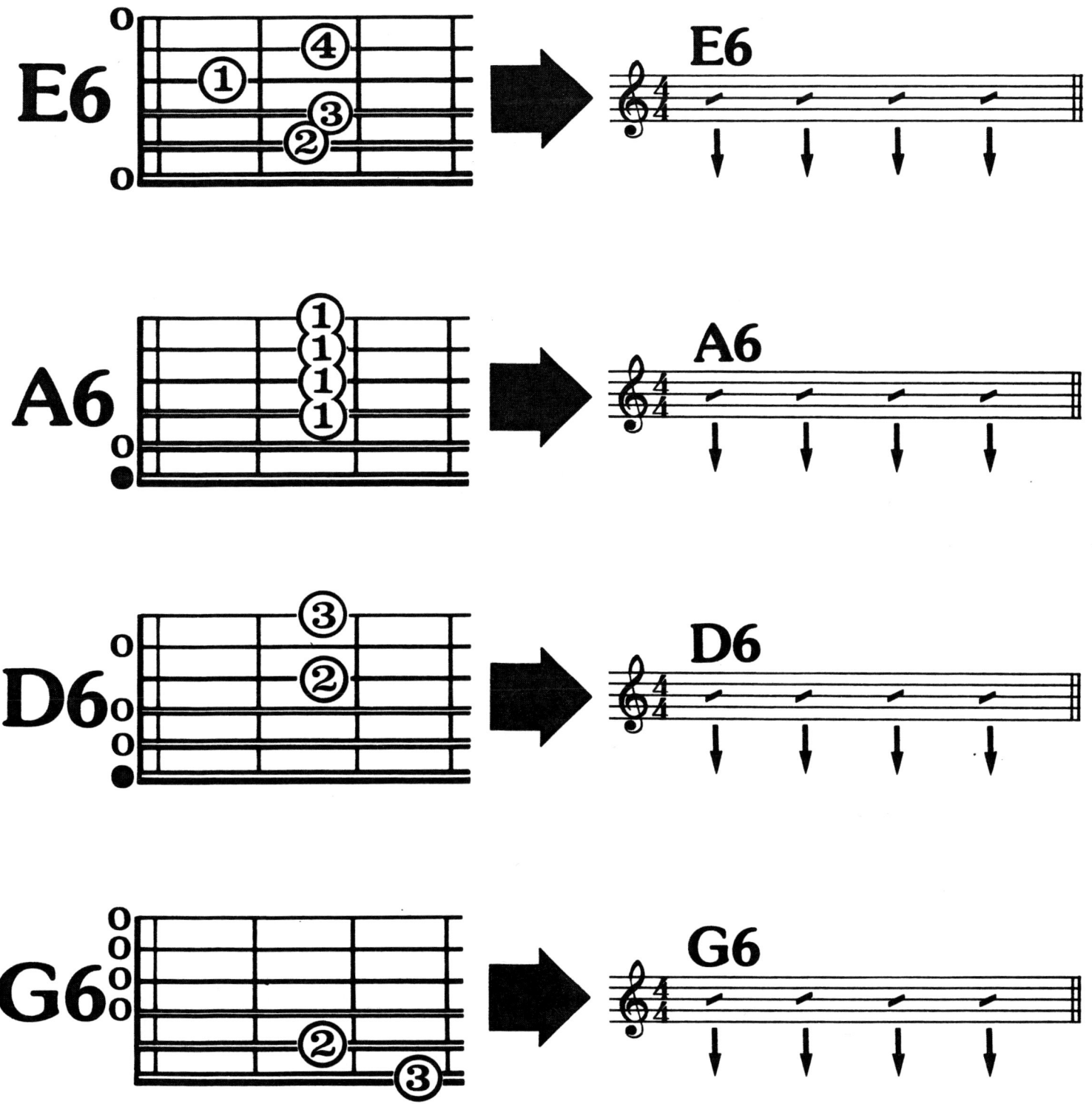

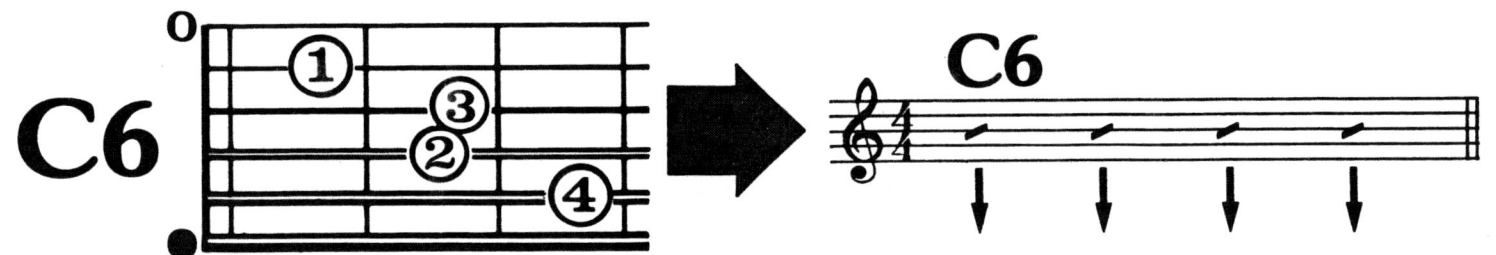

MAJOR SIXTH CHORD PROGRESSIONS

MINOR SIXTH OPEN CHORDS

The Minor Sixth is made by combining the Minor chord and the Sixth chord.

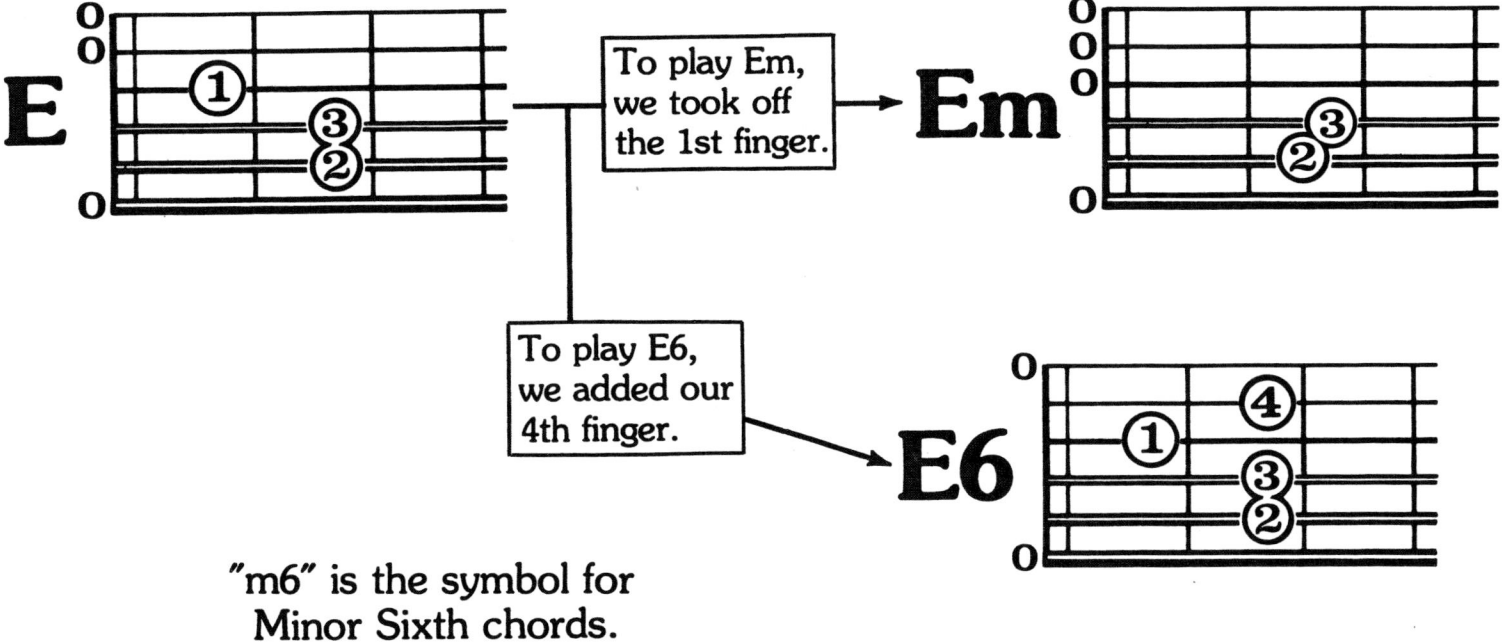

"m6" is the symbol for Minor Sixth chords.

To play **Em6**, take off the 1st finger (making it Minor) and add the 4th finger (making it a Sixth chord).

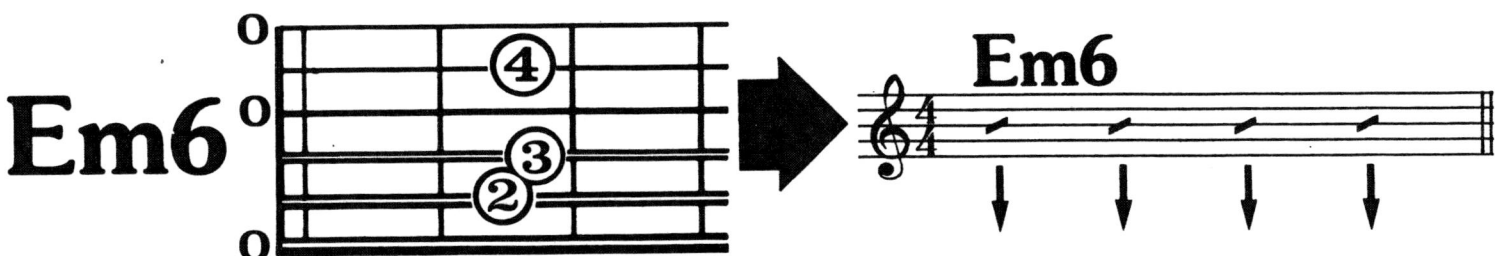

If you can, use this logic to figure out **Am6** and **Dm6**.

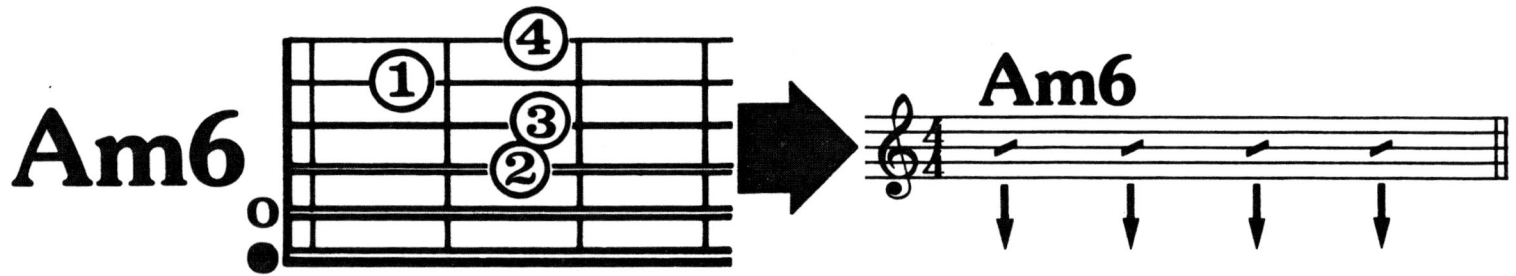

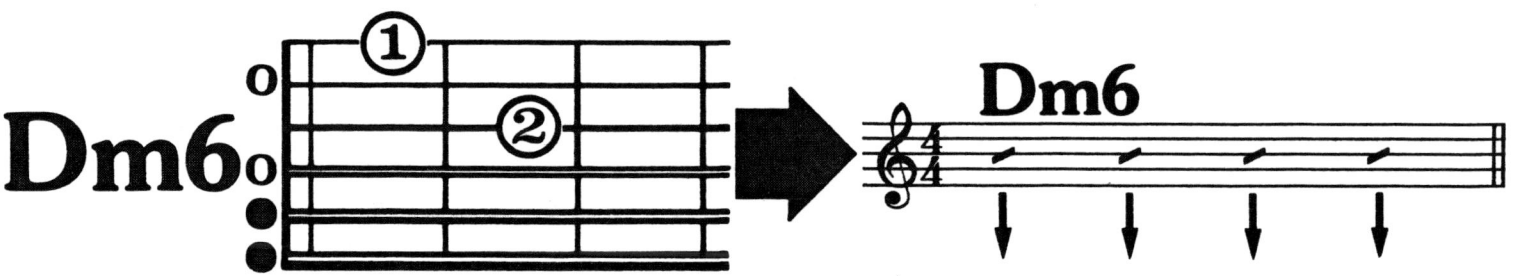

CHORD REVIEW

E	A	D	G	C	
Em	Am	Dm			
E7	A7	D7	G7	C7	B7
Emaj7	Amaj7	Dmaj7	Gmaj7	Cmaj7	Fmaj7
Em7	Am7	Dm7			
E6	A6	D6	G6	C6	
Em6	Am6	Dm6			

MINOR SIXTH CHORD PROGRESSIONS

| E6 | A6 | Dm6 | E6 |

NINTH OPEN CHORDS
ADD9 CHORDS

Add9 chords are one of the most popular sounding chords.
Play these add9 chords and relate them to their chord families.

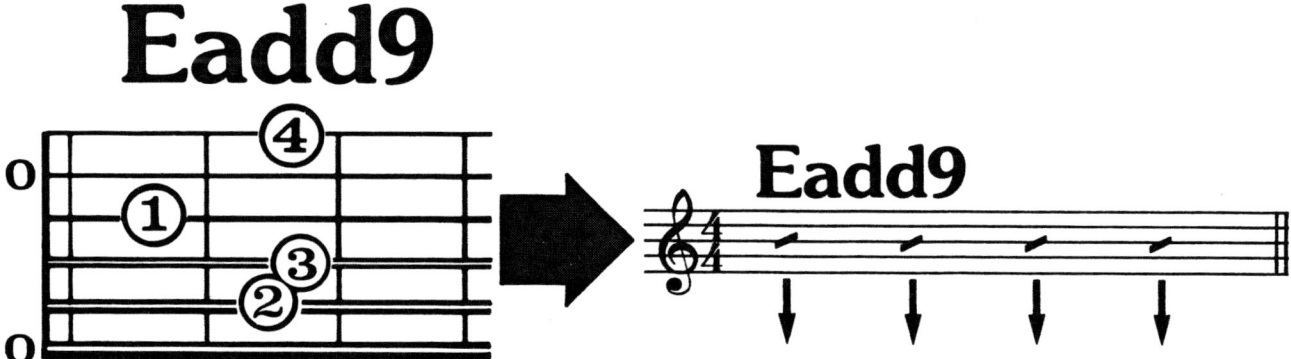

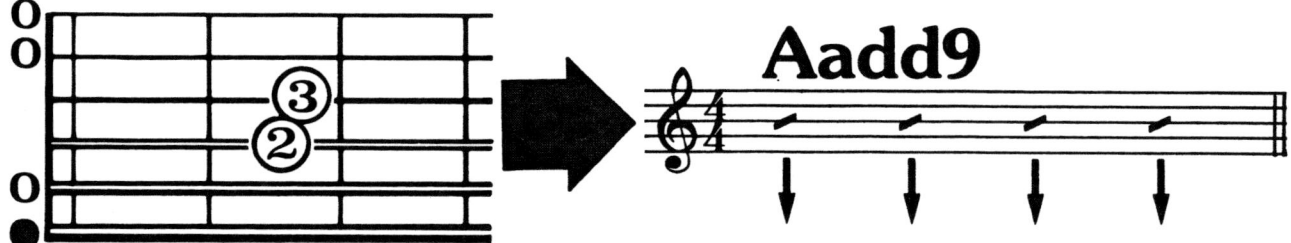

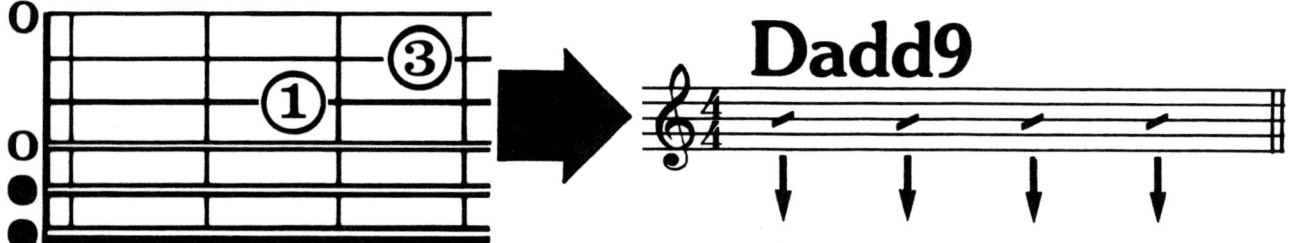

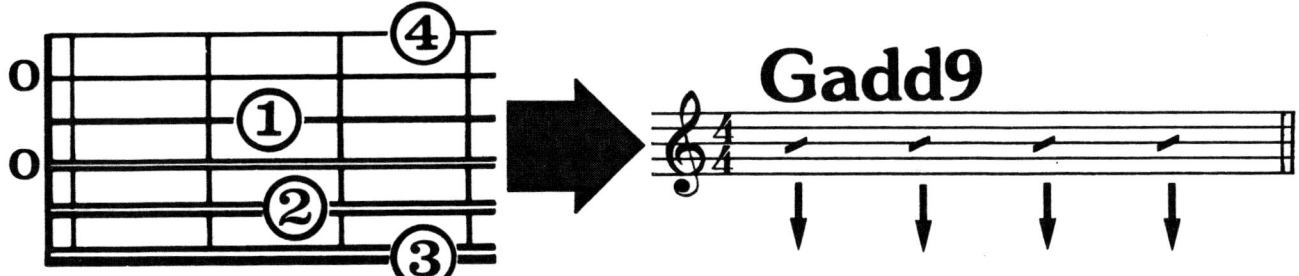

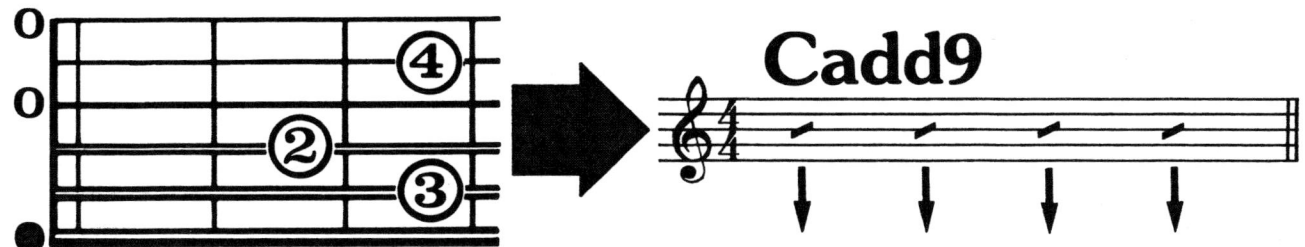

ADD9 CHORD PROGRESSIONS

DOMINANT NINTH CHORDS

To make a Dominant Ninth chord, we simply combine the Aadd9 chord with its Dominant Seventh chord.

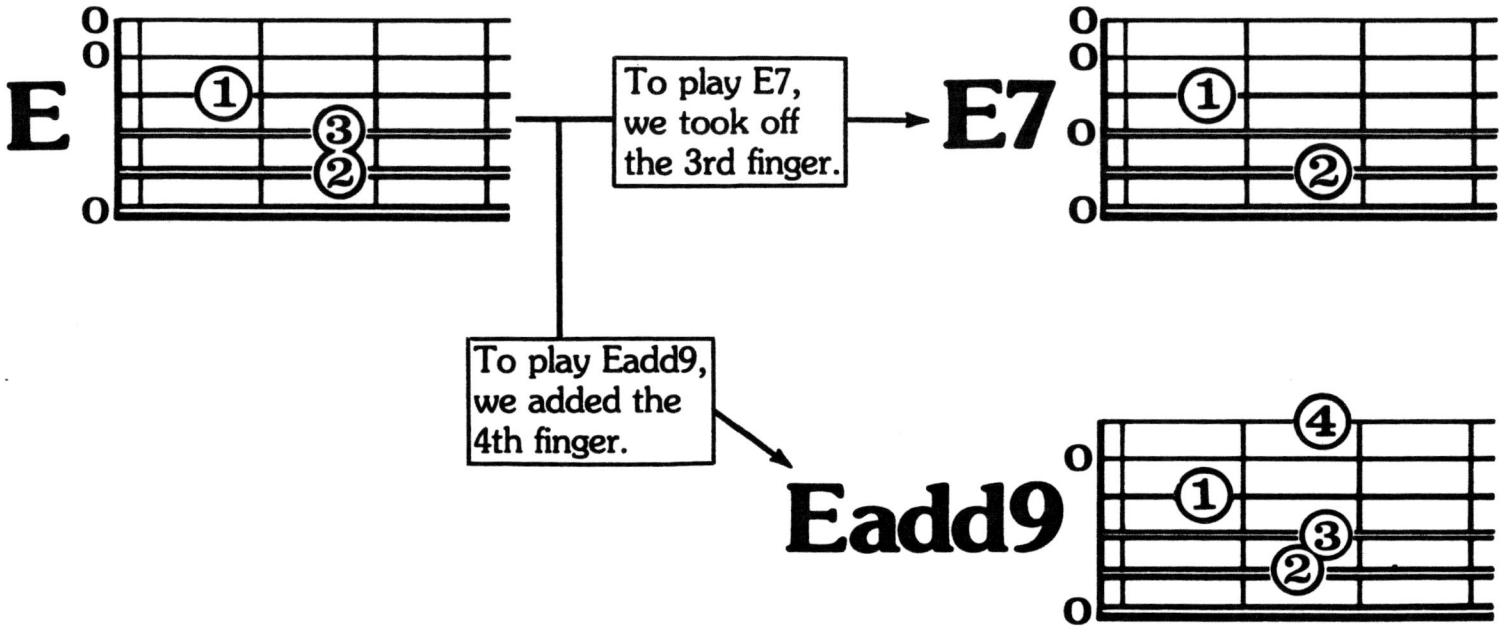

The number "9" is the symbol for a Dominant Ninth chord.

To play *E9,* take off the 3rd finger and add the 4th.

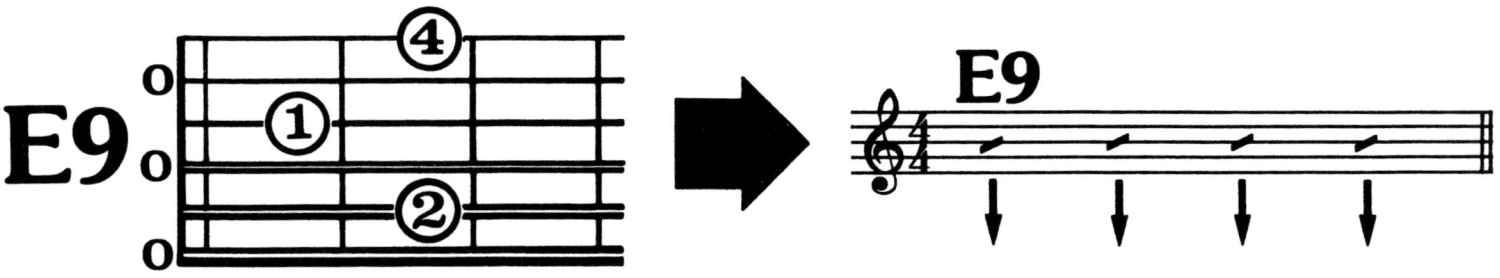

Now use this line of thinking to play **A9, D9, G9,** and **C9.** Once you've tried it, check your chords against the following diagrams. (Note: You'll have to change your fingering to get the C9 chord.)

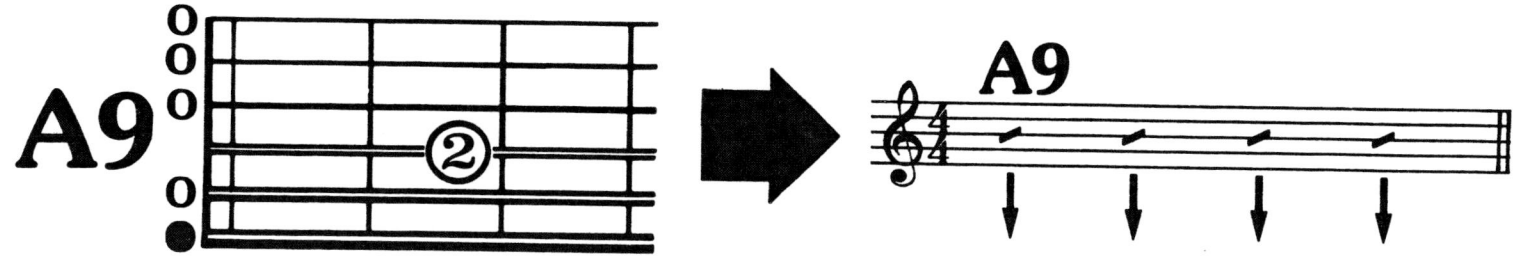

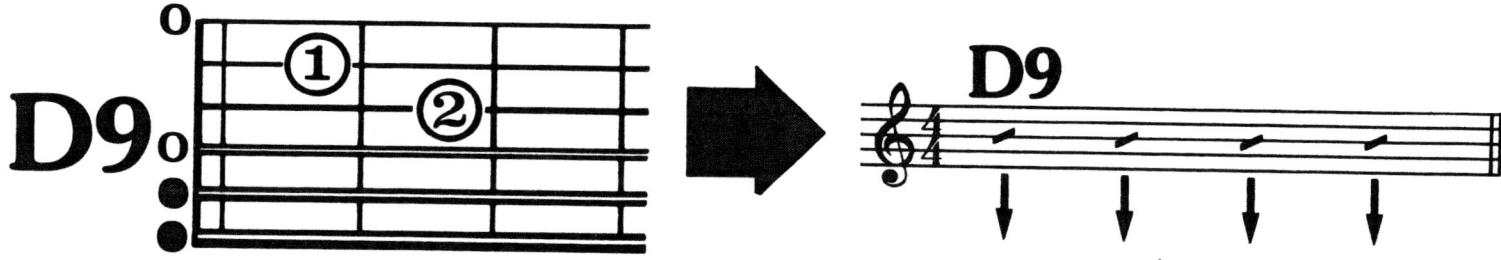

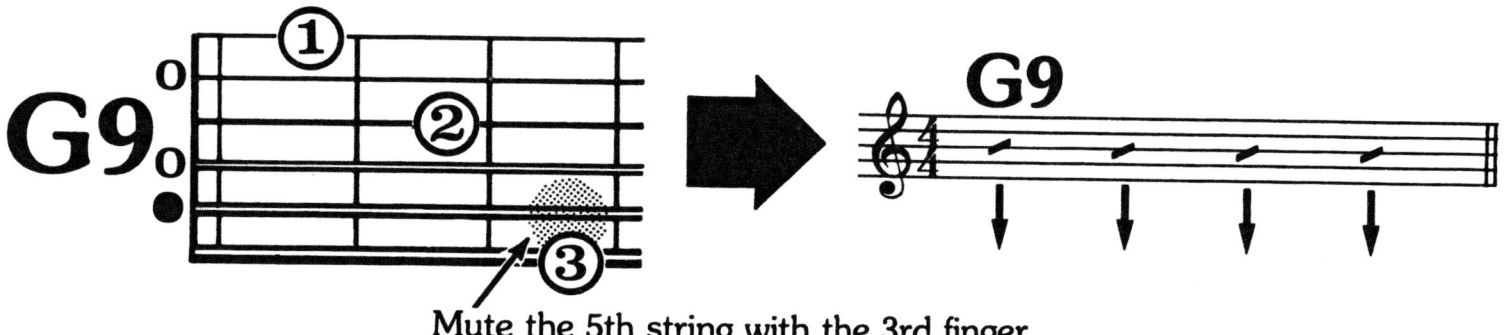

Mute the 5th string with the 3rd finger.

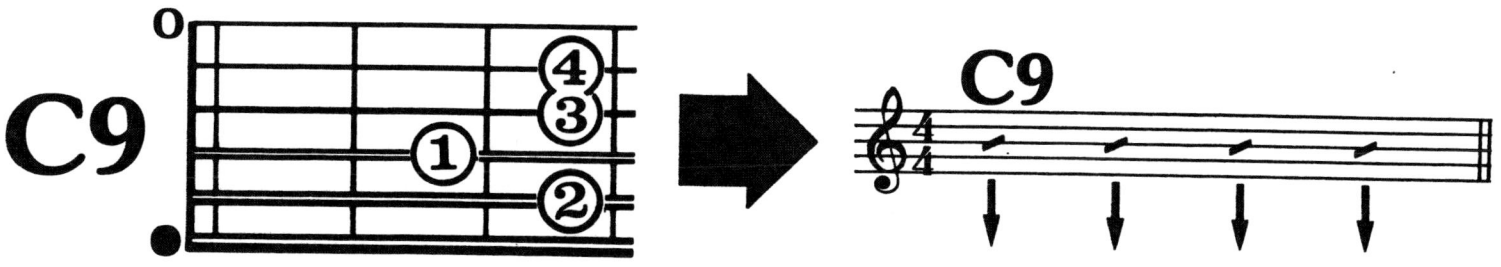

Now try putting them all together.

DOMINANT NINTH CHORD PROGRESSIONS

| E9 | A9 A7 | Dadd9 | D G |

| C | Cmaj7 | C9 | Fmaj7 |

| Am7 | D9 D7 | Gmaj7 | E9 |

| Cadd9 | Em7 A7 | Dm6 | G9 |

| Aadd9 | C9 | Dm7 | E |

SUSPENDED OPEN CHORDS

"sus" (or "sus4") is the symbol for Suspended chords.

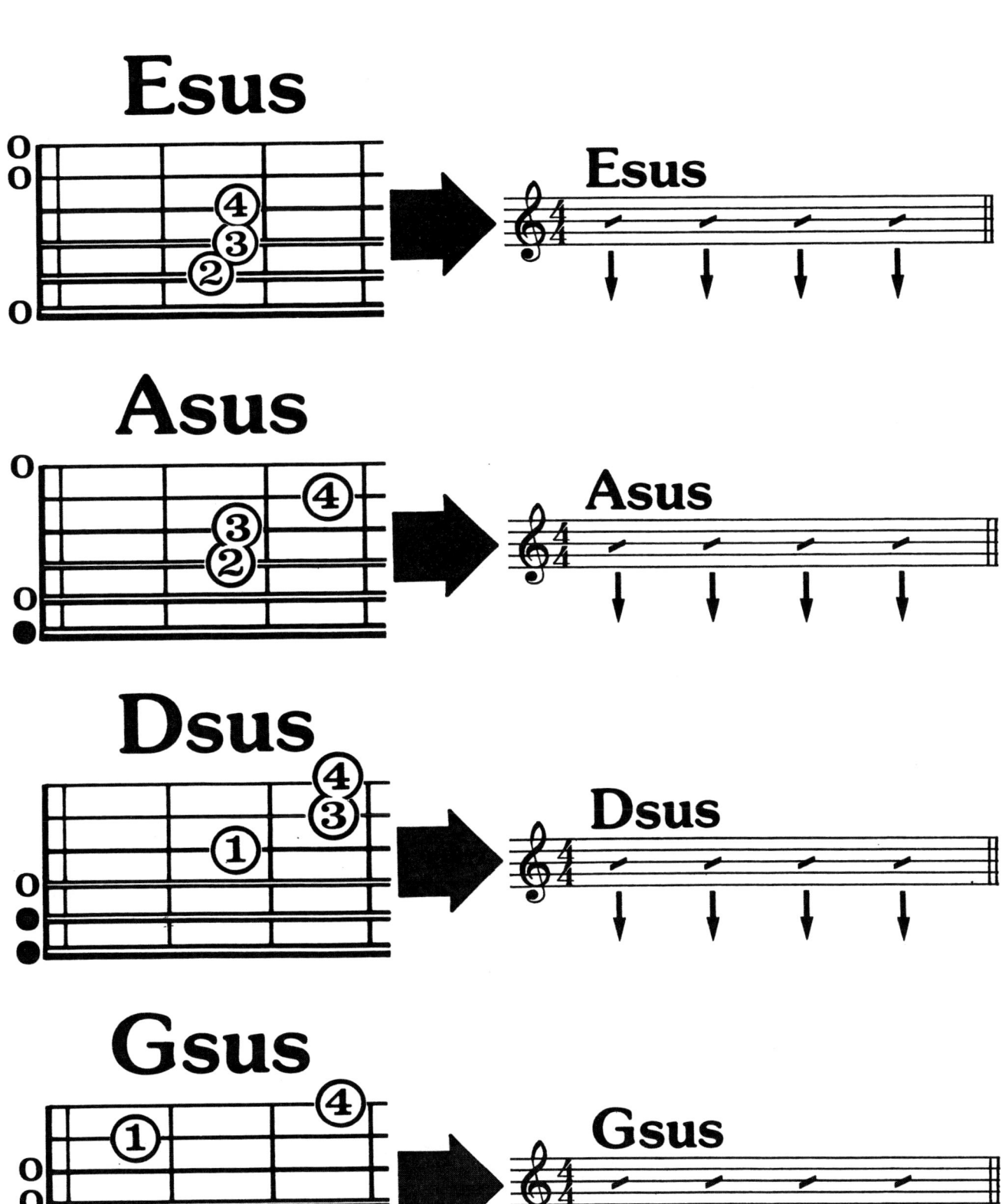

RELATING MAJOR AND SUSPENDED CHORDS

The Suspended chord is usually followed by its Major chord. Notice that only one note is changed to form the Major chord.

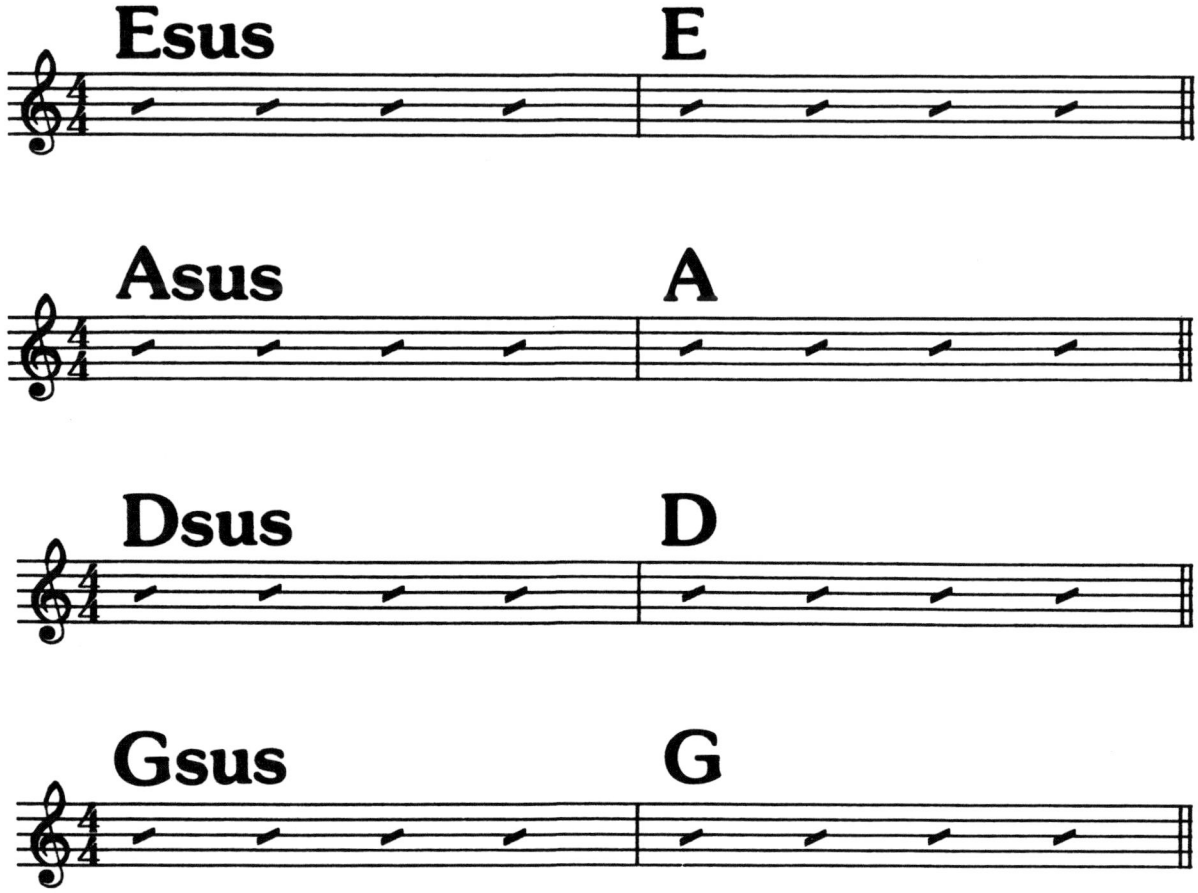

After you've played through all four examples, try playing these chords one right after the other like this—

DOMINANT SEVENTH SUSPENDED CHORDS

In order to play Dominant Seventh Suspended chord ("7sus"), simply add the two chords together like this-

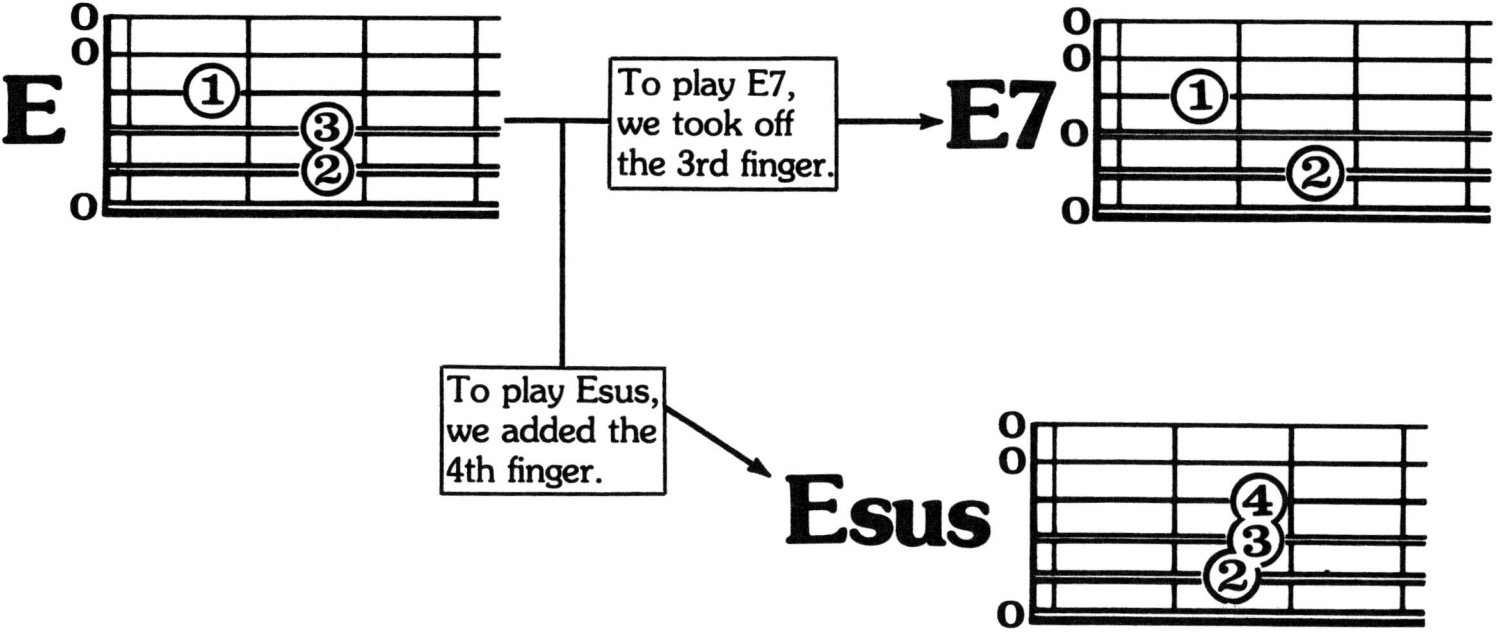

To play **E7sus**, take off the 3rd finger (making it a Dominant Seventh chord) and add the 4th finger (making it Suspended).

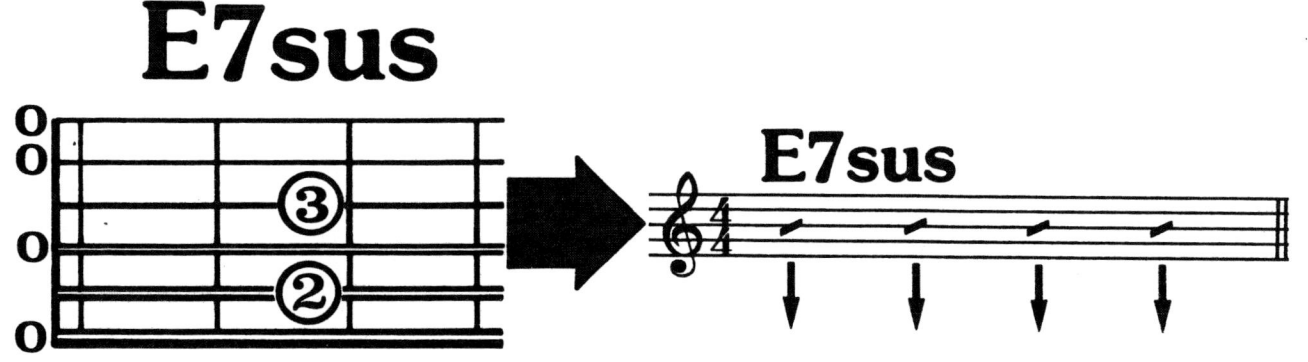

As before, see if you can figure out **A7sus**, **D7sus**, and **G7sus**. Here they are. ⇨

35

A7sus

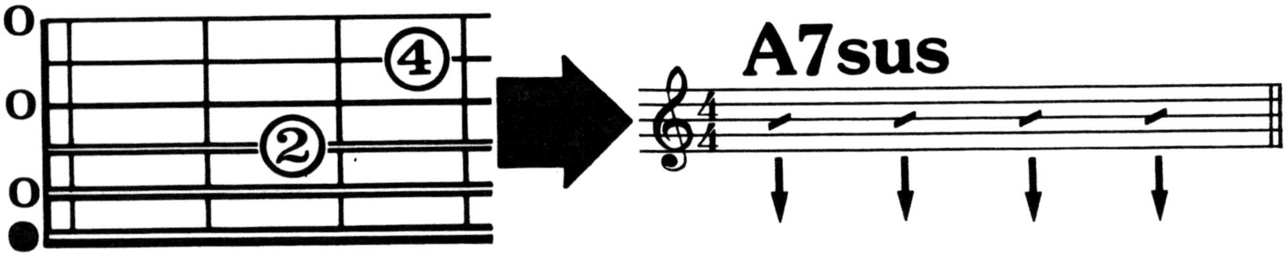

D7sus

G7sus

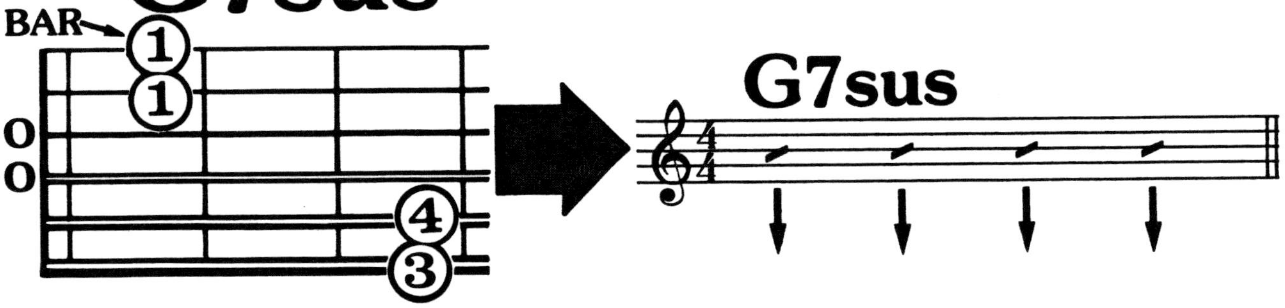

Just like Suspended chords, the 7th Suspended chords are usually followed by their related chord.

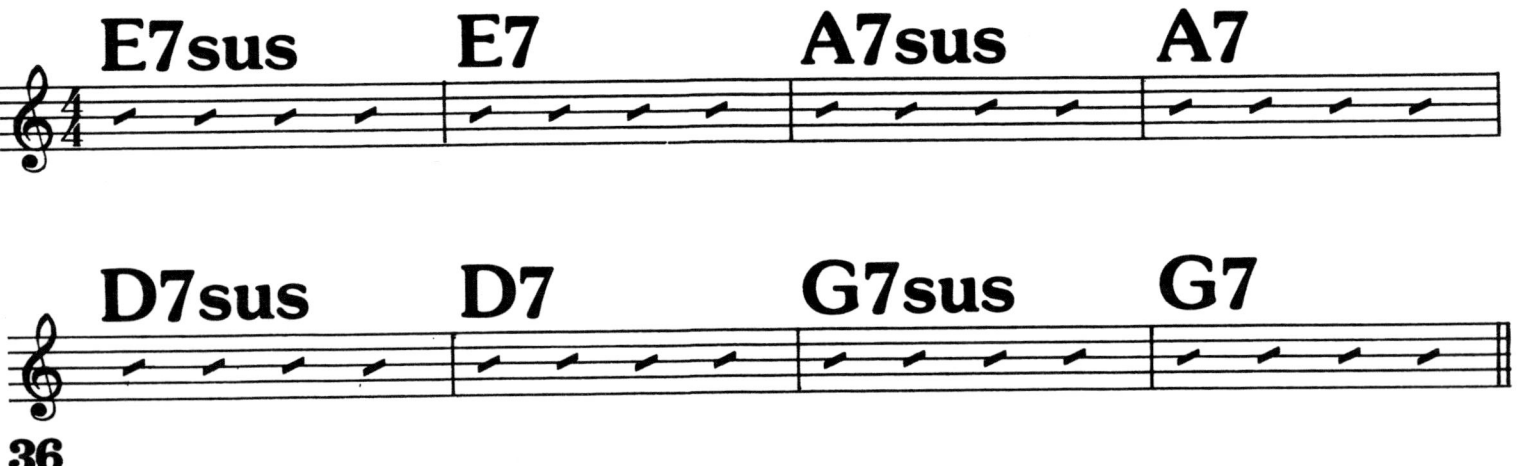

SUSPENDED CHORD PROGRESSIONS

Here are some popular progressions using Suspended chords.

Em | A7 | D7sus | D7

Asus | A | E7sus | E7

D | Dsus | A7sus | A7

C | Dm7 | G7sus | G7

Cadd9 | C | Esus | E

This is an example of a 7sus chord moving to a chord other than its related Seventh chord.

A7sus | Am7 | Gsus | G

DIMINISHED OPEN CHORDS

"o" is the symbol for Diminished.

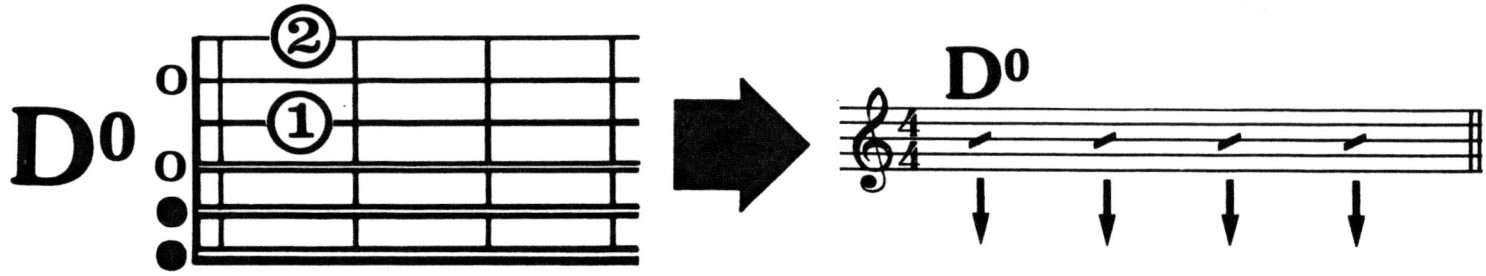

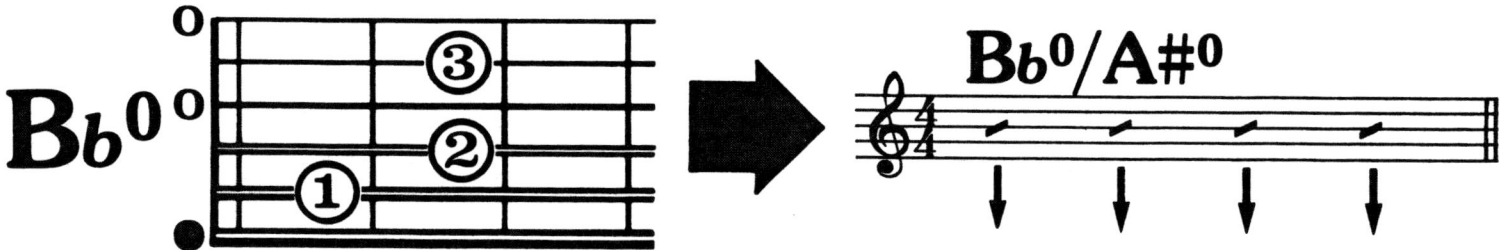

Diminished chords can be used as an effect between their related Major chords...

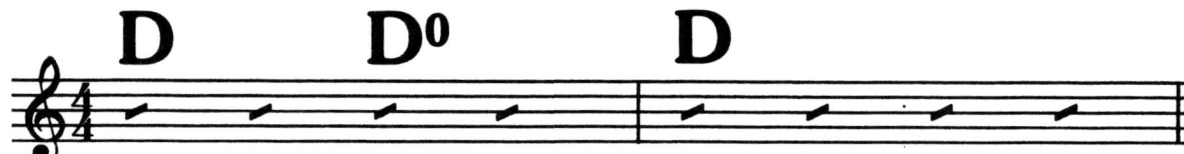

...or between two other chords.

AUGMENTED OPEN CHORDS

"+" is the symbol for Augmented.

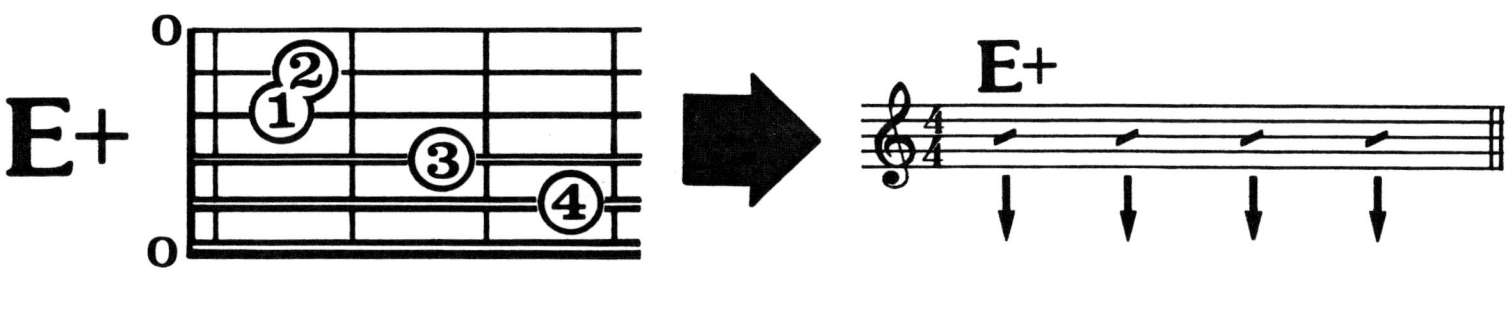

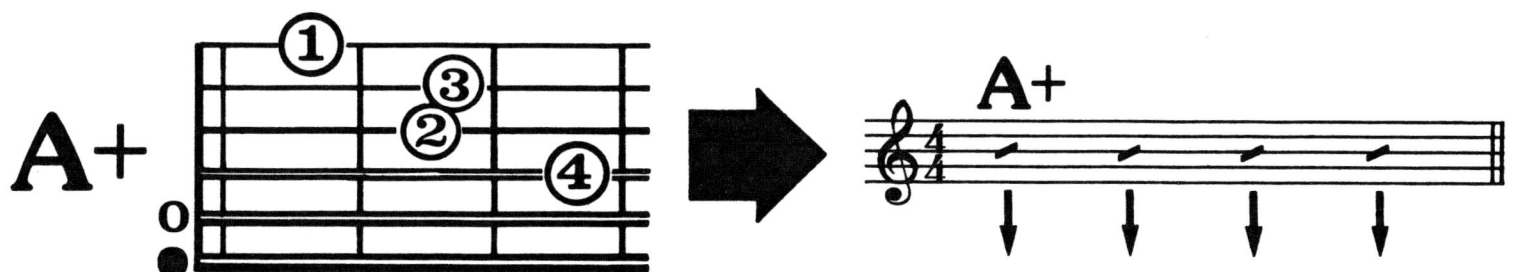

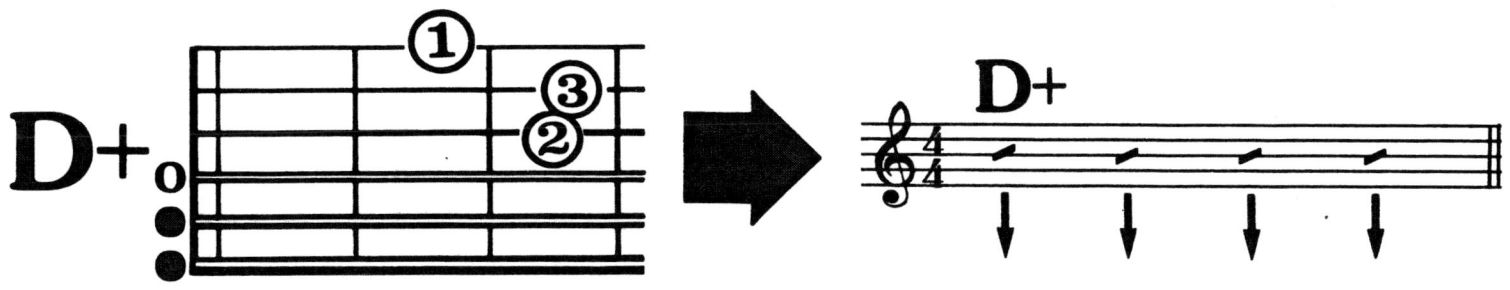

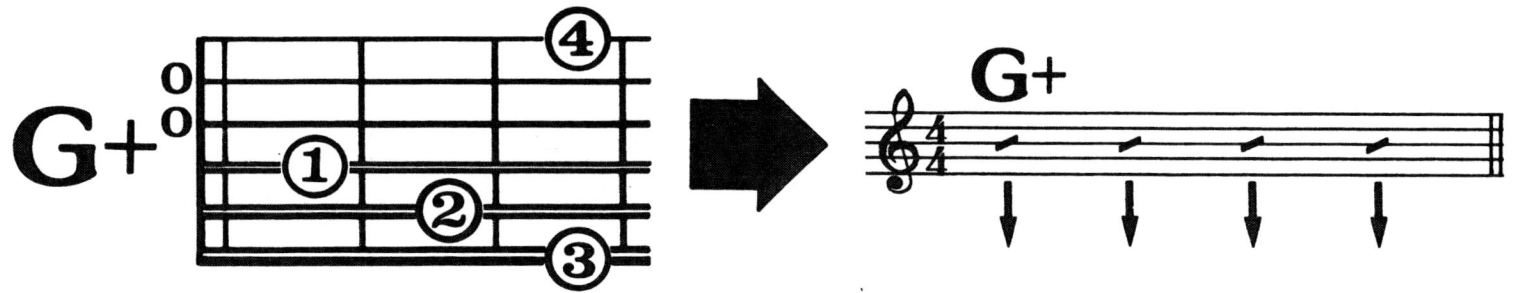

Although these chords are usually used to connect other types of chords, playing them together will help you remember them.

AUGMENTED CHORD PROGRESSIONS

Here are some popular chord progressions which use the Augmented chord.

MASTER CHORD REVIEW
(Chord Families)

Here is a chart of every chord in this book. Test your ability by playing through each family (vertically) and each chord type (horizontally). Once you can do that, it's time for more strums and progressions.

FAMILY →	E	A	D	G	C	(Other)
Major	E	A	D	G	C	—
Minor	Em	Am	Dm	—	—	—
Dominant Seventh	E7	A7	D7	G7	C7	B7
Major Seventh	Emaj7	Amaj7	Dmaj7	Gmaj7	Cmaj7	Fmaj7
Minor Seventh	Em7	Am7	Dm7	—	—	—
Major Sixth	E6	A6	D6	G6	C6	—
Minor Sixth	Em6	Am6	Dm6	—	—	—
Add9	Eadd9	Aadd9	Dadd9	Gadd9	Cadd9	—
Dominant Ninth	E9	A9	D9	G9	C9	—
Suspended	Esus	Asus	Dsus	Gsus	—	—
Seventh Suspended	E7sus	A7sus	D7sus	G7sus	—	—
Diminished	—	—	D°	—	—	B♭°/A#°
Augmented	E+	A+	D+	G+	—	—

RIGHT-HAND RHYTHM STRUMS

The four slashes per measure do not necessarily mean four down-strums. They are used to show time passing. Four slashes, then, could apply to any strum.

NOTATION

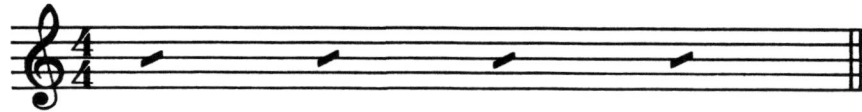

These ten strums are examples of the kind of right-hand possibilities that exist. Even though they go from simple to intermediate, any one of them can stand on its own.

❶ FOUR DOWN STRUMS

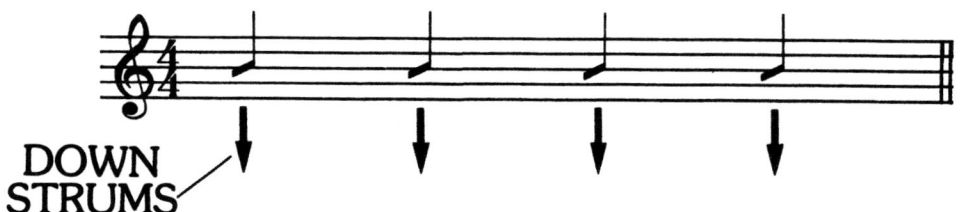

DOWN STRUMS

❷ ADDING UP STRUMS

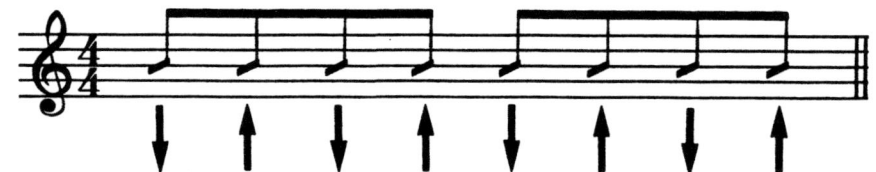

DOWN AND UP STRUMS

When you strum down, play every note in the chord.
When you strum up, play most of the upper (skinny) strings.

42

❸ DOWN AND UP VARIATION

This is perhaps the most common up and down variation. Try making up some of your own variations by putting the up-strum on different beats.

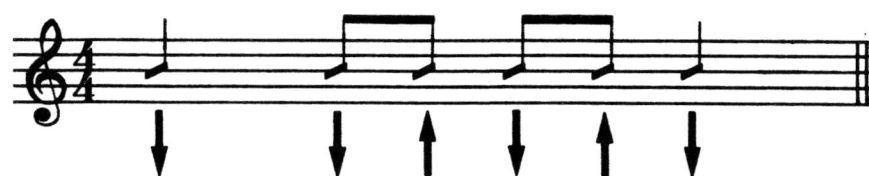

❹ THE TIE

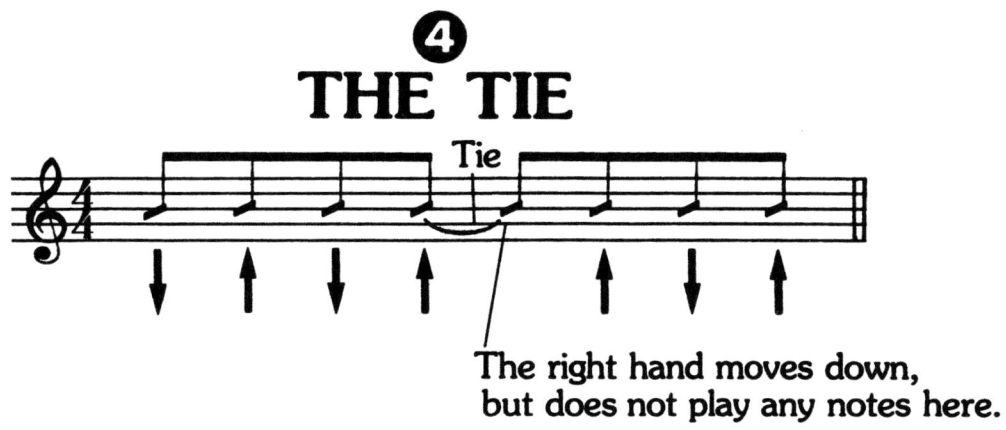

The right hand moves down, but does not play any notes here.

❺ TIE VARIATION

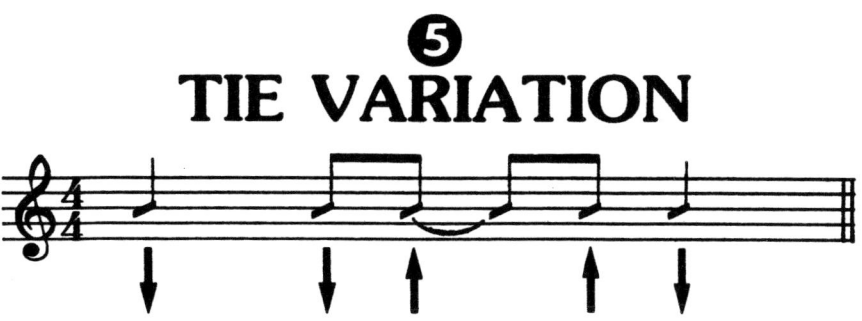

❻ THE SHUFFLE

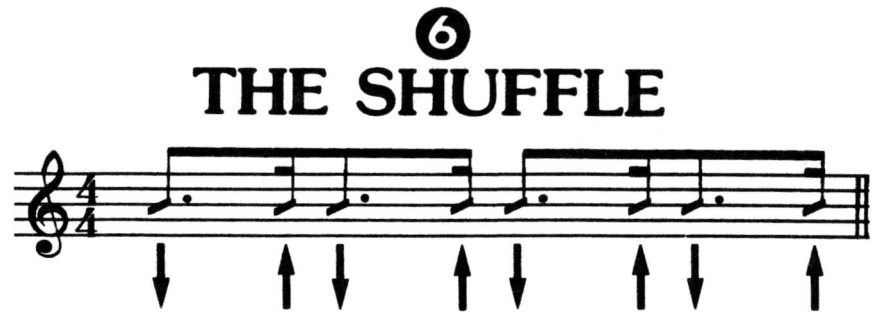

This "Shuffle" feel can be applied to all of the previous strums.

❼ THE PUSH STRUM

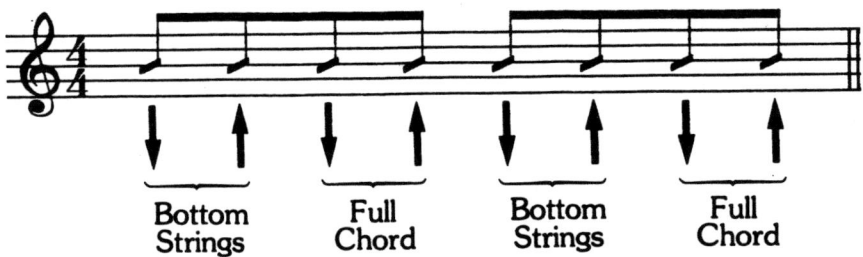

The "Push-strum" can be used with any combination of up and down strums.

❽ THE 2-4 CHOKE

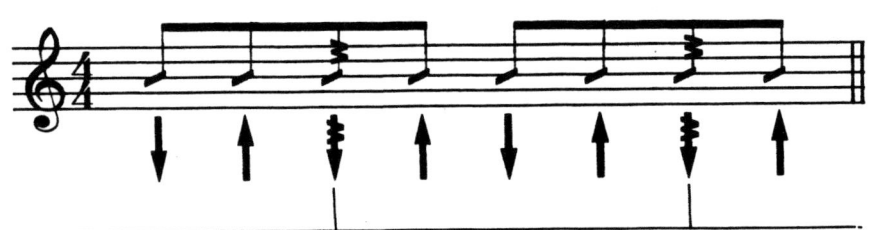

Choke the strings here by strumming through the chord and then immediately stopping the sound with the side of your right hand.

❾ THE 2-4 CHOKE TIE

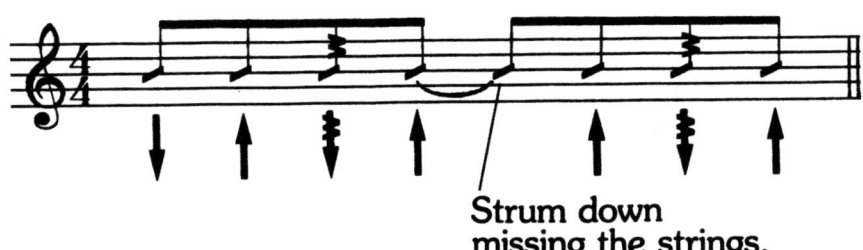

Strum down missing the strings.

❿ 3/4 TIME (WALTZ)

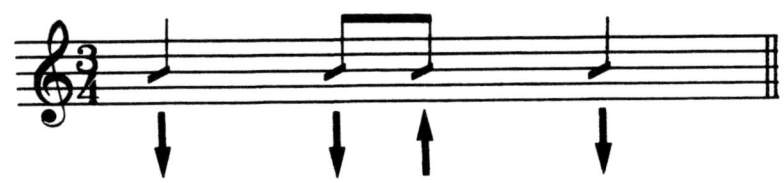

You can play this 3/4 time strum with any chord progression that has one chord per measure.

"OPEN CHORD" PROGRESSIONS

These chord progressions are good examples of popular ways in which open chords are put together.

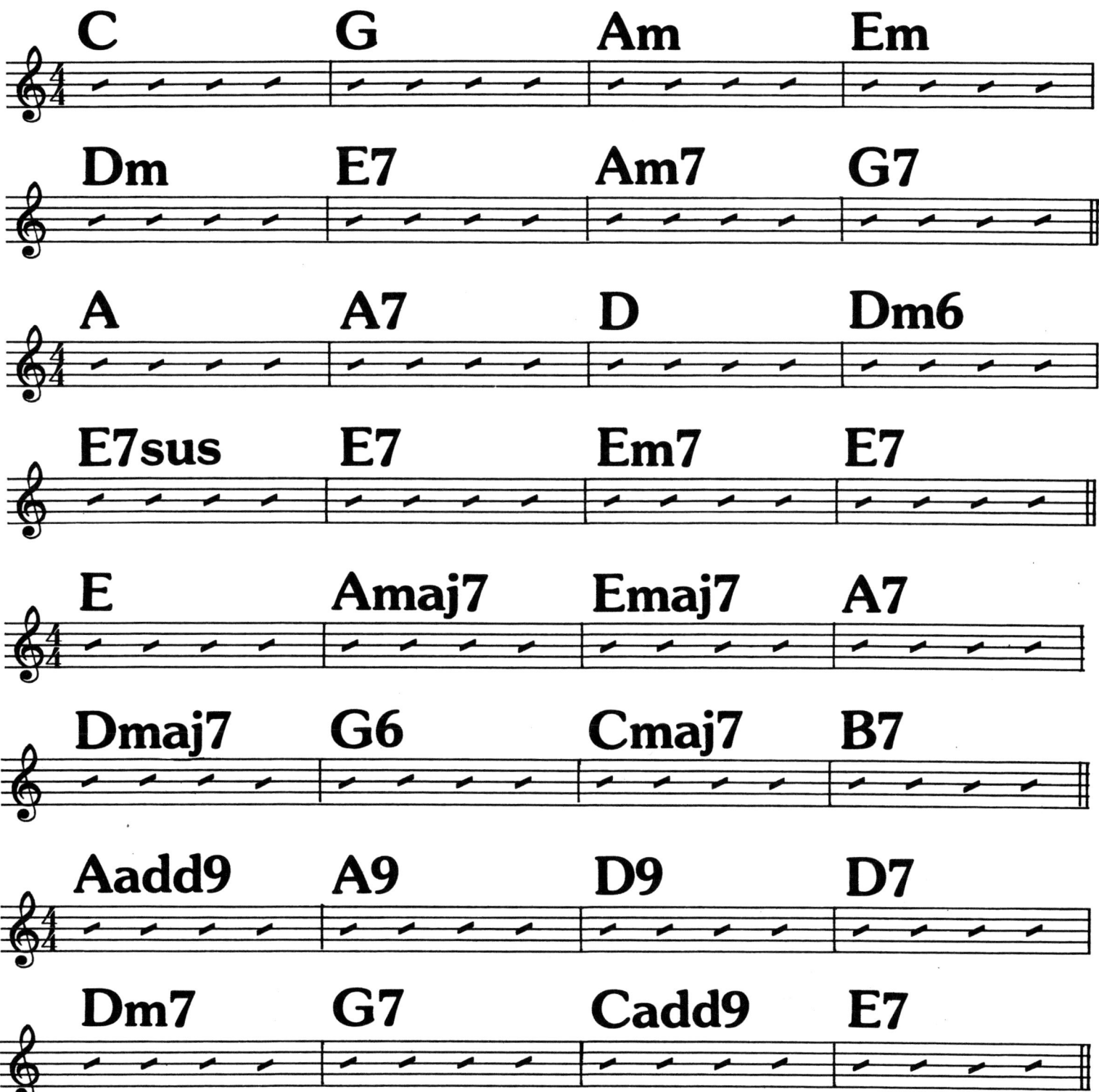

BASIC CHORD THEORY
(What the Numbers Mean)

Why is a C6 chord a C6? What does the number mean?

If we take a Major scale and give a number to each scale degree, we can understand where the numbers come from.

C MAJOR SCALE

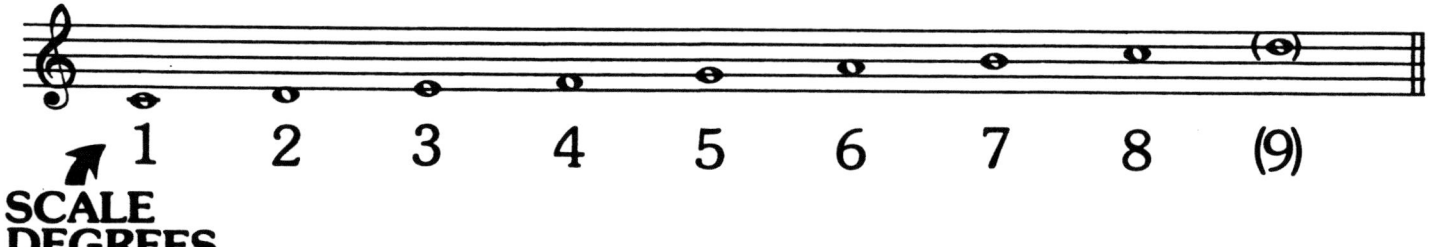

A **Major** chord is made up of the 1st, 3rd, and 5th of the scale. The C Major chord would look like this-

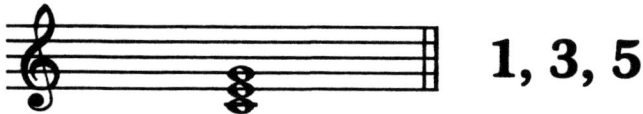

1, 3, 5

To make a **Minor** chord, we would simply lower or flat (♭) the 3rd. This is why only one note changes when we go from Major to Minor.

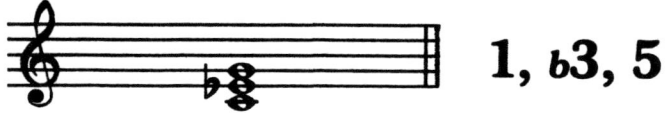

1, ♭3, 5

To play a **Sixth** chord, we add the sixth note of the scale to the chord.

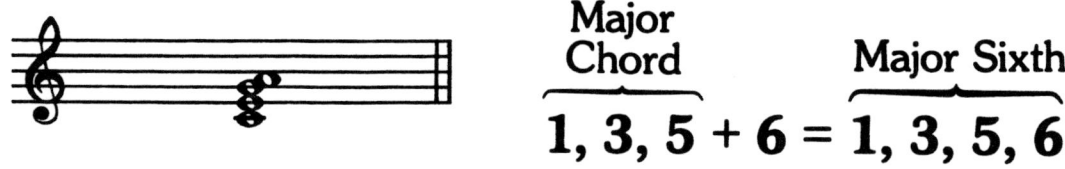

Major Chord: 1, 3, 5 + 6 = Major Sixth: 1, 3, 5, 6

$$\overbrace{1, \flat3, 5}^{\text{Minor Chord}} + 6 = \overbrace{1, \flat3, 5, 6}^{\text{Minor Sixth}}$$

To play a **Major Seventh** chord, we add the 7th scale degree.

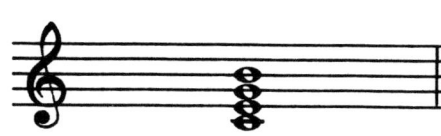

$$\overbrace{1, 3, 5}^{\text{Major Chord}} + 7 = \overbrace{1, 3, 5, 7}^{\text{Major Seventh}}$$

A **Dominant Seventh** chord differs from a Major Seventh chord in that it has a lowered or flat (♭) 7th.

$$\overbrace{1, 3, 5}^{\text{Major Chord}} + \flat7 = \overbrace{1, 3, 5, \flat7}^{\text{Dominant Seventh}}$$

$$\overbrace{1, \flat3, 5}^{\text{Minor Chord}} + \flat7 = \overbrace{1, \flat3, 5, \flat7}^{\text{Minor Seventh}}$$

A **Suspended** chord replaces the 3rd with the 4th tone of the scale.

1, 4, 5

$$\overbrace{1, 4, 5}^{\text{Suspended Chord}} + \flat7 = \overbrace{1, 4, 5, \flat7}^{\text{Dominant Seventh Suspended}}$$

A **Ninth** chord adds the ninth scale degree which is the same as the 2nd scale degree an octave (8 notes) higher.

$$\overbrace{1, 3, 5}^{\text{Major Chord}} + 9 = \overbrace{1, 3, 5, 9}^{\text{Add9}}$$

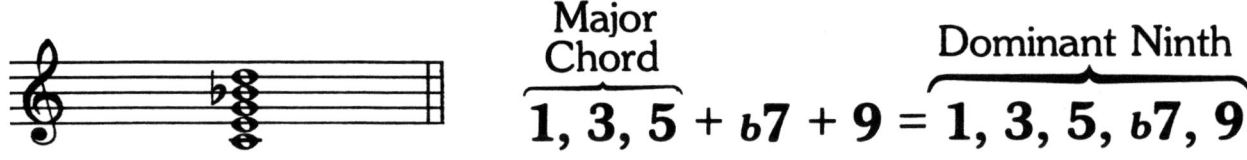

$$\overbrace{1, 3, 5}^{\text{Major Chord}} + \flat 7 + 9 = \overbrace{1, 3, 5, \flat 7, 9}^{\text{Dominant Ninth}}$$

The **Diminished** chord looks like this-

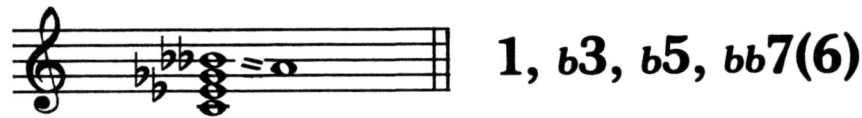

$$1, \flat 3, \flat 5, \flat\flat 7(6)$$

The **Augmented** chord has a raised or sharp (#) 5th.

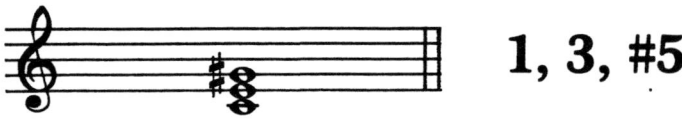

$$1, 3, \#5$$

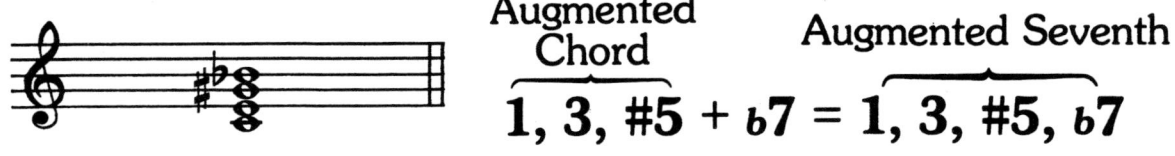

$$\overbrace{1, 3, \#5}^{\text{Augmented Chord}} + \flat 7 = \overbrace{1, 3, \#5, \flat 7}^{\text{Augmented Seventh}}$$